ELEVATE &
EMPOWER

INSIGHTS ON PERSONAL GROWTH, RESILIENCE, AND TRANSFORMATION

FEATURING 10 INSPIRING BUSINESS LEADERS

Published by Prominence Publishing

www.Prominencepublishing.com

ISBN: 978-1-990830-65-5

Table of Contents

Table of Contents

"What lies behind us and what lies before us are tiny matters compared to what lies within us."

–Ralph Waldo Emerson

Introduction

I'm thrilled to present to you a remarkable collection of wisdom, inspiration, and hard-won insights from ten extraordinary individuals. *Elevate and Empower: Insights on Personal Growth, Resilience and Transformation* is more than just a book—it's a roadmap for navigating life's challenges and emerging stronger on the other side.

The inspiration for this book came from a simple yet profound realization: there's a real need for books that don't just inspire, but also empower readers to take actionable steps towards personal growth and resilience.

I envisioned creating a resource that people would turn to not only for motivation but also for practical guidance in navigating life's challenges. The goal was to compile a collection of authentic stories and hard-won wisdom from individuals who've walked the path of personal transformation.

This anthology is the result of that vision - a carefully curated set of insights from remarkable individuals who've faced adversity, embraced change, and emerged stronger. It's designed to be more than just a good read; it's a toolkit for personal evolution, a source of strength during tough times, and a catalyst for positive change in our readers' lives.

By bringing together these incredible authors and their experiences, we hope to create a ripple effect of empowerment and growth that extends far beyond the pages of this book. We encourage you to reach out and connect with the authors to continue the conversation.

The authors featured in this anthology come from diverse backgrounds and experiences, yet they are united by their courage to face adversity head-on and their willingness to share their journeys with us. From corporate leaders to military veterans, educators to entrepreneurs, each contributor brings a unique perspective on what it means to grow, adapt, and thrive in the face of life's obstacles.

As you delve into these pages, you'll discover:

- Savana Maxon's powerful journey from imposter syndrome to authentic leadership

- John R. Robertson's insights on staying true to your values and leading with integrity

- Adela Vladutoiu's framework for women leaders to adapt to change and find opportunity in adversity

- Emily Marquis's practical approach to building resilience habits from the inside out

- Peggy Beneby's inspiring story of overcoming personal tragedy and professional challenges

- Glen Henderson's guide to building a bulletproof mindset

- Floyd McLendon Jr.'s seven principles of excellence, forged through his experiences as a Navy SEAL

- Judith Field's practical advice on mastering the art of public speaking

- Jeff Katz's touching and inspiring account of parenting a child with special needs

Throughout these chapters, you'll find a wealth of practical strategies, thought-provoking insights, and deeply personal stories that illuminate the path to personal and professional growth. Whether you're facing a career transition, grappling with self-doubt, or simply seeking to elevate your life and leadership, you'll find guidance and inspiration within these pages.

What sets this anthology apart is not just the quality of advice offered, but the authenticity and vulnerability with which it is shared. These authors have opened their hearts and minds, offering us a glimpse into their struggles and triumphs. In doing so, they remind us that resilience is not about avoiding challenges, but about how we face them and grow through them.

Elevate and Empower is more than a collection of stories—it's an invitation to transform your own life. It's a reminder that within each of us lies the power to overcome, to grow, and to make a positive impact on the world around us.

Thank you to our incredible authors for their bravery, wisdom, and generosity in sharing their experiences. And thank you, dear reader, for embarking on this journey of growth and empowerment with us.

Here's to elevating ourselves and empowering others!

Suzanne Doyle-Ingram

Publisher,
Prominence Publishing

Facing the Edge:
The Emotional Ups and Downs of Growth

By Savana Maxon

Imagine standing on the edge of a diving board, the shimmering pool beckoning below. Your heart pounds a frantic rhythm against your ribs, mirroring the chaotic symphony of doubts playing in your mind. "What if I misjudge the height and bellyflop?" the voice of hesitation sneaks in. "What if jumping in is the easy part, but once I'm in the water, my brain forgets how to do the whole 'not sinking' thing?"

This is the deceptive adversary of imposter syndrome, manifesting in its ever-changing and various ways. For some, that's the challenge of unfamiliar tasks and responsibilities. For others, it's the nagging voice downplaying their achievements, saying, "It was just luck," or "Anyone could have done that," preventing them from experiencing growth and self-discovery.

But it is in the moment when we pause, breathe deeply, and silence those inner doubts that we find the strength and confidence to make the plunge. That space between the leap and the landing is a transformative journey, allowing us to realize our true potential. When we do land, we emerge stronger and more confident.

It's an adventure worth taking.

Unmasking Imposter Syndrome

As I stood in front of the mirror, my reflection stared back at me, a mixture of excitement and anxiety in my eyes. I was ready to be vulnerable and share my personal struggles publicly, hoping to inspire those attending. My heart pounded as I rehearsed unseen parts of my story, yet, as I stumbled over my words, doubts crept in like a heavy fog.

"Who am I to talk about exposing imposter syndrome?" The hesitation inside my head taunted, reminding me of my long-standing companionship with skepticism, which kept intruding into my life uninvited.

In a broken household with a father struggling with substance abuse and a mother fighting her own battles, I had no choice but to assume the role of caretaker from a young age. My father's moods were unpredictable, shifting like a summer storm. One moment the sun was shining, the next, his anger would erupt, leaving me trembling and speechless in its wake. The silence that followed was the worst part, heavy with unspoken tension and a looming fear of the next outburst.

This constant ebb and flow resulted in me constantly needing to be on guard. These experiences left me in a state of confusion, leading me to doubt my value and identity. I perfected the art of concealing my hidden turmoil, crafting a facade of normalcy that seemed suffocating.

Despite experiencing personal and professional successes and substantial growth, I acknowledged that these internal demons occasionally resurfaced. However, through healing and increased awareness, I've learned to reframe my thoughts and gain the courage to disclose my past. It wasn't just my own growth and healing; it also involved supporting clients, colleagues, and friends, all of whom trusted me enough to be vulnerable about their struggles with fear and doubt. Their accounts deeply connected with mine, pushing me to confront my fears for both myself and those who depended on me.

My sense of duty became particularly clear one day when I stepped into a client's office. Let's call him Jim. His space was meticulously organized, with clean lines and shiplap walls rebuilt from reclaimed wood. Lush plants thrived in the bright light, and every document had a designated place in labeled cabinets or the internal database. Despite their efficient system for sending out proposals to potential clients and projects, I noticed a significant gap: there was no mechanism for following up to address questions or scheduling. The proposed work didn't provoke the next step or a reply.

When I pointed this out, it became evident that there was more to the story. We delved deeper, exploring the challenges he faced in his follow-up process. How comfortable was he with reaching out again? What emotions arose during this stage? He entrusted me with his fear of rejection and aversion to hearing the word "No."

This revelation was startling as I reflected on the years of bids and completed work that could have generated substantial income had there not been this operational gap. Delving deeper, I uncovered that my client's apprehension stemmed from his experiences proposing bold ideas to the original founder, only to face dismissive reactions. These encounters had seeded self-doubt, which grew unchecked over time. His method of handling bids and proposals significantly hindered his ability to champion necessary changes, despite his team's consistent success.

Once the moment arrived for him to step into the position of the organization's new leader and CEO, his initial enthusiasm quickly waned. Despite his successes and growth, he found himself increasingly burdened by the dependence of processes, team members, and clients on his involvement. This dependency consumed his time, ensnaring him in day-to-day operations. His lingering doubts and fears about relinquishing control to focus on broader strategic initiatives stifled his ability to muster the courage needed to foster innovation.

One significant concern was the reluctance of middle management to embrace beneficial technologies. Whenever he introduced new ideas, he faced resistance. Middle managers were comfortable with the status quo and were hesitant to adopt changes that could disrupt their familiar routines. This reluctance created friction as he struggled to convince them of the long-term benefits of technological advancements.

Additionally, he encountered unanticipated difficulties in enforcing significant policies. His colleagues, who should have been his allies in these initiatives, expressed similar reservations. They feared that implementing new strategies would lead to failures that could jeopardize the company's stability. This constant push-and-pull between the desire for advancement and the apprehension of failure created a persistent conflict.

Changing Jim's strategy for bids and projects achieved far more than just ensuring potential clients weren't lost due to not following up; not only did it streamline processes, but it also allowed him to separate himself from the rejection he had avoided for so long. This shift in mindset reignited his sense of empowerment and success. His transformation sparked a chain reaction, uplifting his team and organization. By demonstrating vulnerability and sharing his personal struggles with imposter syndrome, my client created a ripple effect within the organization. His willingness to confront his anxieties and put in place changes inspired his team to embrace growth and push past their own limitations. The enhanced client management process streamlined operations and fostered a mindset of ownership and innovation.

As the weeks passed, I watched in awe as my client flourished in his leadership role. His confidence soared as he tackled challenges head-on, unafraid of rejection or failure. The once immaculate office now buzzed with energy and creativity, a stark contrast to the sterile environment I had first encountered.

It was several weeks later, as I sat across from him in a strategy meeting, that he turned to me with a smile that reached his eyes. "Thank you," he said, gratitude clear in his voice. "I never realized how much my fear was holding me back until you helped me see it."

I smiled back, sensing a surge of pride in his transformation. "You did the hard work," I replied. "I just helped you see the path forward."

Together, we continued to plan and innovate, each meeting building upon the last as our partnership flourished.

As we finished another productive session, I couldn't help but feel a profound sense of fulfillment. Observing my client triumph over his fears and fully embrace his true potential was a gratifying outcome. It was a reminder that sometimes the greatest challenges we encounter are the ones within ourselves, waiting to be overcome.

When I left the office that day, I reflected on my journey battling feelings of inadequacy. It was an ongoing battle, but witnessing the transformation in my client inspired me to continue pushing forward, gradually and steadily.

The journey to conquer imposter syndrome was not an easy one, but it was a necessary one. As I stood on my diving board, ready to leap into uncharted waters, a surge of confidence and determination flooded within me. The doubts that once clouded my mind dissipated, replaced by a fierce resolve to embrace the challenges ahead. With a deep breath, I dove headfirst into the unknown, trusting in my abilities and believing in the power of development and self-discovery.

Navigating through the murky depths of my fears and insecurities, I embraced each obstacle as an opportunity to learn and grow. Every setback became a stepping stone toward greater resilience and inner strength. Day by day, doubt lifted from within me.

When the day came to stand before a crowd of eager faces and share my story of overcoming imposter syndrome, I felt a rush of adrenaline coursing through me. The words flowed from my lips, carrying with them the wisdom and courage I had gained on my journey. As I looked out at the sea of hopeful gazes before me, I saw reflections of my past hardships and accomplishments. I shared not only a narrative of my own transformation but a demonstration of the human spirit's strength and evolution.

At that specific moment, I realized that my journey was not only about my own growth but also about inspiring others to confront their fears and embrace their true potential. The audience's reactions mirrored the transformation I had witnessed in my client. Their movements, inspirations, and readiness to take their own leaps of faith were evident.

As I concluded my speech, I felt an overwhelming sense of contentment. I had come full circle, from battling my own doubts to helping others conquer theirs. Though the journey continued, my perspective had shifted. Fear no longer loomed large, replaced with a sense of determination. I welcomed the challenges ahead with open arms, knowing that each one would bring me closer to becoming the best version of myself.

As I left the stage, a deep connection with everyone present filled me with a consuming energy. We were all on this journey together, learning and growing, making progress bit by bit. With every story shared, every fear faced, and every triumph celebrated, we were collectively moving toward a brighter, more empowered future.

Section 2: The Journey of Self-Discovery

The process of self-exploration is essential for aligning your passions and purpose with your career goals. It plays a critical role in personal fulfillment and professional success, as it helps inform decision-making and develops resilience. This journey can uncover hidden talents and interests, providing you with a clearer understanding of yourself and aiding in navigating your career path with confidence.

Your Personal Journey

During my formative years, I encountered difficulties that made me prioritize the feelings of others, causing me to develop coping mechanisms. It was when I met an insightful counselor who helped me break down my defenses, uncovering their profound influence, that I made a breakthrough in understanding how my past encounters shaped my reactions and responses that I carried into my present interactions and relationships.

My professional narrative transformed when I integrated my personal story. The process was challenging and eye-opening, pushing me to face my identity and long-held fears. Discovering myself led me to uncover my genuine passions and align them with my career aspirations. It demonstrated how my experiences influenced my current strengths and areas to develop.

Advice for Others Embarking on the Path of Self-Exploration

1. **Explore Your Inner Self:** Intentionally set time to reflect on your feelings and experiences through journaling, a powerful tool for identifying patterns and passions.

The deeper I ventured into self-discovery, the more enthralled I became by the quiet power of introspection. Journaling, once a neglected corner of my life, blossomed into a cherished ritual. It became a sanctuary—a space where thoughts and feelings flowed freely, unburdened by the fear of judgment. Spontaneous ideas found a landing place within its pages, captured alongside moments of sudden inspiration or clarity. Emotions, once tangled and elusive, began to reveal themselves under the scrutiny of the pen. As I wrote, buried aspects of myself surfaced, forgotten treasures emerging from the dust. Untangling the interwoven threads of experiences and present emotions, a profound understanding of my inner self began to take shape.

2. **Expand Your Horizons:** Be open to new experiences and activities, whether it's trying out a new hobby or diving into a different field of study. Stepping outside your comfort zone can lead to discovering hidden talents and passions you never knew you had.

I made the decision to end a ten-year relationship, leaving a gaping hole where a part of myself and an identity I clung to so tightly used to be. Collecting the fragments, I recognized that I had transformed into more of a "wife" and "mother" than the lively individual I used to be. Rediscovering that forgotten self became my mission. A forgotten dream list surfaced, a relic from a younger, bolder me. It wasn't a grand manifesto but a collection of whispers from a past life. Some entries might seem trivial to outsiders, but each held the promise of rediscovering a lost piece. Learning to blow glass, a spark of artistic yearning. A one-on-one, up close and personal, VIP experience behind the scenes feeding a giraffe at our zoo, a childhood fantasy, come true. Embracing the position of a mentor, a chance to impart the wisdom I had amassed. Even a simple act of kindness, like paying for someone's groceries, seemed to ignite a tiny flame again.

Gratitude washes over me now, not just for the crossed-off items but for the even longer list that remains. It's a constant reminder, a whisper amidst the chaos of life: my dreams still matter. This journey of rediscovery is far from over, but with each completed task, I feel a piece of myself returning.

3. **Seek Support and Guidance:** Don't let fear hold you back from asking for help and support from mentors, counselors, or trusted loved ones. Their perspectives can offer valuable insights and encouragement as you navigate the complexities of self-discovery. Even when it may be hard and challenging, do what you can to be honest, trust, and lean on other people's beliefs and views of you.

The past etched itself into me, a constant reminder in the form of a guarded silence. Opening up resembled the exposure of a raw nerve, a vulnerability that I fiercely shielded. Stepping outside was a terrifying act, attending events a hurdle I wasn't sure I could clear. Yet, with each pushed boundary, a sliver of the ice around my heart began to melt.

Conversations became a bridge, tentative at first, then flowing. Questions replaced the deafening silence I held onto for a considerable amount of time. It seemed as if I was taking apart a stronghold, uncovering fragments of myself that I had concealed. The air grew lighter, exchanged for a sense of connection I never thought possible. For the first time, strangers did not surround me, but people who saw themselves reflected in my story. Shared experiences became the mortar that built a bond stronger than anything I had known.

One specific memory stands out, etched in my mind like a turning point. A new counselor sat across from me, the weight of countless diagnoses hanging heavy in the air. The condition known as Post Traumatic Stress Disorder was a term that had become a familiar refrain, a label I wore with a weary acceptance. After sharing my story, a heavy silence settled in the room. I braced myself, waiting for the same verdict. "Can I share my opinion?" she finally asked, her voice gentle. My stomach clenched. I mentally prepared myself for the diagnosis as she started to speak. "You are a textbook example of..." she started, and my mind raced to fill in the blank: Stress Disorder. But the words that left her lips were a revelation. "Post-Traumatic Growth."

Tears streamed down my face as I repeated the words: "Post-Traumatic Growth." The room seemed to shimmer, and in that moment, I understood. It wasn't simply about trusting others, it was about trusting myself. The path forward wouldn't be easy, but the fear had been replaced by a newly discovered sense of empowerment. Making my story known is no longer an act of vulnerability but an affirmation of the strength I've discovered within.

4. Celebrate Milestones: Take the time to acknowledge and celebrate your achievements, no matter how small they may appear. This will reinforce a positive self-image and keep you motivated on your journey.

For months, my mind was a cluttered attic, filled with echoes of "should haves" and past missteps. The gleaming trophies of major milestones felt like distant mirages, while the smaller victories—the daily steps forward—went unnoticed and uncelebrated. It wasn't until a heart-to-heart with a close friend that the cracks in my perspective began to show. As I spoke, words tumbled out, laced with frustration. I recounted receiving a prestigious award, a recognition that should have felt like a triumphant peak. Yet, personal challenges had almost robbed me of the joy of attending the ceremony.

Sharing that story, a wave of realization washed over me. For as long as I could remember, my gaze, always fixed on the expectations of others and circumstances beyond my control, had been missing the most crucial element: myself. I had nearly missed celebrating my own resilience, the strength it took to reach that summit.

Now, each week brings a new adventure, a chance to step out of my comfort zone and connect with those around me. Whether it's nurturing a friendship or volunteering at a community event, the focus has shifted. The path unfolds before me, paved with the intention to make a positive impact. This newfound awareness fills me with a quiet pride, a joy in the journey itself, and a deep appreciation for the small victories that propel me towards my dreams.

The Ripple Effect of Personal Growth

Impact on Others

Personal growth and empowerment extend beyond the individual, influencing those around you. When you embrace your journey, you become a guiding light of possibility for colleagues, clients, and loved ones. Your transformation can inspire others to pursue their own paths, creating a chain reaction of positive change.

My self-discovery journey unfolded, and its effect on others grew clear. Colleagues and loved ones noticed a shift in my demeanor, a newfound confidence that radiated from within. I became a source of inspiration for those around me, as my story of resilience and transformation resonated with so many who had faced their own struggles.

One colleague, who had always seemed reserved and unsure of herself, approached me one day with a glimmer of hope in her eyes. She opened up to me about her own struggles with insecurity and doubt, expressing how my journey had given her the courage to explore her passions and pursue her long-held dreams. As we sat together, sharing stories and offering support, I realized the transformative effect of individual development in action.

My personal transformation was no longer about me; it was about building a community of support and encouragement where each person could thrive and showcase their true brilliance. As I became more open about my journey and vulnerabilities, I observed others becoming empowered to share their own. We formed a powerful network through personal and professional relationships. Conversations sparked motivation, empowering each other on our growth journeys.

Together, we uplifted each other, navigating the waters of self-discovery. And through this interconnectedness, our impact multiplied, surpassing what one person could achieve alone.

Impact on Others

Never underestimate personal growth. It can have a substantial effect that extends beyond changing an individual. Like a pebble thrown into calm water, it creates ripples that reach and transform the surrounding water. Our path toward growth possesses the capacity to encourage and uplift those around us. I have felt this with imposter syndrome. The ways it showed up in my life and my experience of facing and overcoming its impact sparked a positive chain reaction in all areas of my life. This encompasses my personal life, my professional journey, and my role as a parent.

Illustrating the Ripple Effect

Like a stream finding its way through rocky terrain, self-improvement flows through lives, carving a path that influences diverse aspects. My transformation into a leadership role was pivotal in driving organizational growth from 67 to 300 employees and expanding our presence to 36 states within just 2 years, despite the challenges posed by the pandemic. This expansion was a direct result of our team's steadfast dedication to nurturing a culture that fosters empowerment.

Our focus on cultivating a supportive and motivating work environment facilitated the successful implementation of an innovative performance management system. This platform significantly boosted productivity and accountability across the organization, playing a crucial role in our company's success and development. These efforts have defined a new level of progress and advancement.

The influence of personal development on leadership and organizational success is profound. Remember Jim? His courage in acknowledging and confronting his anxiety about rejection led to significant changes. By implementing a new follow-up system, his company secured a major contract, showcasing their capabilities and inspiring his team to adopt similar strategies. This sparked a culture of innovation and accountability, encouraging initiative and suggestions for how improvements could be made.

Through our commitment to an empowering culture and effective performance management, we have created a thriving, dynamic workplace that continues to inspire and achieve remarkable outcomes.

Your Personal Story Matters

Sharing your unique experiences can profoundly impact both your own growth and those around you. Embracing and accepting your narrative while inspiring others fosters connections built on shared purpose, enriching your experiences, perspectives, and journey.

Navigate your path with courage and curiosity, and allow your story to evolve into a guiding force of hope and inspiration for those who are watching and listening. Your life story, struggles, and triumphs serve as a testament to the transformative power of individual growth and the boundless potential within each of us.

Take the leap into the depths of your own being. Dive fearlessly, make a splash, and uncover your extraordinary narrative—it's waiting to be shared.

About the Author

Savana Maxon isn't your average operations guru. She's a culture architect, renowned for building thriving workplaces at Lucro Consulting (her leadership fueled a remarkable 300% revenue surge in year two!) and through her own firm, Sonder Operations. Savana's secret weapon? Infectious leadership and innovative solutions that empower businesses. Her hands-on approach helps teams navigate challenges and elevate their dynamics.

But Savana's passion extends beyond consulting. As a Fractional Leader, Speaker, Facilitator, and Amazon Bestselling Author, she empowers leaders and entrepreneurs at scale, enabling them to cultivate thriving cultures and achieve their missions. A staunch advocate for diversity, equity, and inclusion (believing that inclusion fuels innovation!), Savana serves as a Global Ambassador for Women in Tech and holds board positions with two non-profits dedicated to fostering opportunities for future leaders.

Savana isn't driven by accolades (though hers are impressive: Circle of Influence Honor, Accomplished under 40, and two Women of the Year Awards); what truly fills her cup is making impactful connections.

Connect with Savana to unlock your business's potential:

Website: www.sonderops.com

Email: savana@sonderops.com

Looking to expand your network or explore mentorship opportunities?

LinkedIn: www.linkedin.com/in/savanamaxon

Instagram: @savanamaxon (for a more casual touch)

Authentic Leadership: Staying True to Your Values and Leading With Integrity

By John R. Robertson

Jonathon's job required him to move to Canada. While his home in the UK had many similar practices, the one that frequently caught him off guard was the number of times people would ask him how he was doing.

His first visit to Walmart was a memorable one, including for those of us who heard the story about it.

It was late afternoon when he walked through the front doors of the store, and immediately was met by the greeter. "Good morning, Sir, how are you today?"

Jonathon's response was perfect. He looked at the man and responded, "I am so glad someone has asked. It has been a terrible day so far; in fact things have gotten worse as the day has unfolded. I see you have chairs over there, may we go sit down as I am so glad you have asked *how I am doing*. I really need to offload some things."

As you can well imagine, the greeter's look of horror and shock greeted Jonathon. The number of "umms" and "ahhs" plus the sheer awkwardness caused Jonathon to backpedal and go easy on the greeter. He smiled at him and told him he was just having some fun. While the fun might not have been mutual, can you imagine how the greeter would tense up the next time he asked that simple question?

Think about the number of times you and I hear, how are you today? How are you doing? It's exhausting to always be responding with "I'm fine, I'm good" and smile.

To thrive and grow forward is to rethink the thinking. As an example, if you love a hobby, sport or activity, do you really care what other people think? This authenticity is the core of leading well.

To realize genuine authenticity is not just a program one takes. There is no course that gives a magic formula of what to do. But this is already a known truth, isn't it? Knowing more information does not always mean a person is smarter. In the same way, learning more information does not mean a person is more genuine, real, or possess greater integrity. Authenticity is never a one-and-done, as it is something to be lived every moment of each day. This practice happens in all areas of things that matter, whether it is loving someone, staying true to our values, or even just being resilient. Just because you and I have more information, do something once, love someone once, stay true to our values once, or are authentic or resilient once, does not mean that it is forever.

This is like a muscle that must be exercised to remain strong, or it will atrophy. This process of transformation, of exercising and strengthening, is called growth. The truth is that any living thing that is not growing is atrophying.

There is a uniqueness to authenticity because it connects directly with genuineness or realness. The other side of this coin is just as true. Can a person connect to the other who has it all together, where life is fine or good, and their stress is limited to deciding what color clothes to wear? I know I can't.

At the core we are talking about trust, and trust in leadership is not optional. People keep saying that we need to be authentic, vulnerable, and model integrity while staying true to ourselves. Yet so many put on the mask of 'being fine.'

Authenticity and transparency have become less about being real and more like another mask to wear, which is a byproduct of program thinking. Courses, tasks, and expectations get added to an already full plate. Perhaps you've summoned the courage to try authenticity, vulnerability, or even transparency, and wow, you did not see that response coming. The result was a **note to self**: *don't do that again.* Tragically, when this happens, wise humans stop sharing but then get accused of keeping secrets.

The hurdle is we are human <u>beings</u>, not human <u>doings</u>.

Everyone knows that to say one thing and do another is to lack credibility, or perhaps integrity. The influence, which is just leadership, behind authenticity is the credibility that comes from being and doing the same things.

To thrive and lead well is a collage of four facets, where all must be put into practice.

1. Relational currency is the exchange rate of authenticity.

2. Clarify the meaning, especially what it means for you.

3. Define the motivation, the real one.

4. Grow forward—don't try to 'hatch' something.

1. Relational currency is the exchange rate of authenticity.

Without going down a rabbit trail, let's put this into something most of us can relate to (if you've traveled outside your country).

In finance, an exchange rate is the rate at which one currency will be exchanged for another currency. The exchange rate is also regarded as the value of one country's currency in relation to another country's currency. There is no agreement in the economic literature on the optimal national exchange rate policy. Rather, national exchange rate regimes reflect political considerations.

This exact same principle applies in relationships. The difference in the currency value is determined by the recipient, not the one asking.

There are relationships with weak currencies, and then there are those relationships that we would invest in, no matter the cost difference. This currency difference is the vague force in any relationship that impacts rapport, chemistry, credibility, trust, etc. Not understanding this facet can result in the relationship, like a bank account, going into overdraft.

This is most visible when a low relational currency relationship asks another to work on something, do something, or help. They will seldom get an outright "no" as this often just generates reactions from the one who asked. The answer looks more like doing things, including dithering. Saying things like "I am busy right now," or "I'd love to help, but I do not have any extra time." The excuses roll off their tongues. Bottom line, authenticity does not happen. They do not share their real motivation for not being available or willing to assist.

Authenticity requires the willingness to lower one's shield (psychologically, emotionally, spiritually, etc.) to allow the other to see the real person. It is not a mask to paste on but the relief of knowing and being a real person. It is not sharing things that should not be shared but showing who you and I are in a powerful way. When humans feel cared for, we tend to respect the ones who care even more, don't we?

This relational component causes deeper roots, and ironically, the deeper roots allow for more relational currency, which means forgiveness and understanding when a human misses the mark. It is that understanding that when others want to throw stones and point fingers, high currency people lock arms with the other. They protect and support, while others scapegoat.

2. Clarify the meanings, especially what it means for you.

One of the greatest hazards in any relationship is thinking that communication is what is said. It is never what is said but what is heard. It is clarifying, "What do you mean when you say…?"

This happens when leaders get tripped up by thinking that being 'real' is about showing weakness, faults, struggles, and so forth. While it might include these, it is also sharing what is energizing, encouraging, and what one is passionate about. Otherwise, it is merely putting a mask on and thinking people will not see beyond it. Just think of the old Greek theatre masks that we might have seen pictures of, but what's behind it is visible.

One must first clarify the terminology to stay true and lead with integrity. Whether it be thriving, authenticity, or even evaluating. When you say you want to evaluate the best approach, what are the values you are e-value-ating by?

This same principle applies to authenticity. If we do not know what it means and looks like in practice, how can we demonstrate it? It applies to being true to ourselves. What does this mean for you? While most of us have never met a person who says they do not have any integrity, there are those who do not share the definition of integrity we hold. These become more masks to put on like "I'm fine, I'm good, doing well," etc.

3. Define the motivation, the real one.

This is the values statement in a nutshell. Ironically, most humans sense insincerity within a few moments of meeting another person.

There usually tend to be two sets in operation, actual and aspirational. The difference is that when the pressure is on, during those hot-water moments, the real values leak out just like the contents of a tea bag. In organizations and companies, the difference is between the website values or the ones in the brochures and the ones that people operate by in the workplace. These values are expressed by individuals as the values lived, those in our bank statements and day timers. Aspirational values are the ones that we tell people. Authenticity gets tripped up when people look at the person or organization and see that these two types of values don't match. This is often described as people saying that the walk and the talk don't match. This is merely just the theme of integrity that is being highlighted.

Values are motivational preferences. They are not merely ethics, a code of conduct, or some form of 10 Commandments. There is an incredible thing that happens when a person tries to appear genuine. Most humans have an innate intuition or sixth sense, which picks up on this façade. This instinctual feature in humans is to protect our lives, not just safety and well-being. Why would this suddenly be different in any work or other life relationships?

Values motivate initiative. This is not a passive process. They take the initiative to model and practice it on a regular basis. It is not pretend or make-believe, just to put a mask on. That is why real leadership through critical moments requires authenticity, which shines through as integrity.

4. Grow forward—don't try to 'hatch' something.

This is the difference between a gardener who grows things and someone thinking there is a magic wand to make it appear. One of my favorite rants is this issue when it comes to education and training. The thought was that if a person got an education, then they would be able to know what to do. We put people in classrooms and programs, thinking that this is education.

That is like thinking that putting a person in college for two years will make them an electrician, a carpenter, etc. To illustrate my point, would you want me to build your house or wire it all after I have completed one of these programs? I would honestly hope not.

Training is good for thinking and awareness, but education is what happens when we do something with the training and information.

To grow forward and thrive means getting some information and doing some work to define what it looks like as an individual. Then start working with it, practicing it, and refining it. The challenge is most adults fear doing something wrong more than we fear most anything else. Added to that, most people I know are impatient. We want something, we want it now, and if we must wait and persevere, we get frustrated.

Ironically, it is this perseverance and practice that is called resilience. By taking the initiative to practice and be resilient, we get to a point where we can look back to see growth. Values are those motivational preferences that cause us to take the initiative, strengthen our resolve, and have the responsibility to continue living them despite the temperature of the water we might be in or the winds that we might be facing.

All values are short-term costs for long-term benefits. If the value is respect, then the other person may not always like us. Ironically, when they see the respect value shine through, likeability becomes less valuable. This works the same with trust and integrity.

People's perception is their reality. They watch us through their filters to discover our values. This is based on what they see, hear, think, and feel. Authentic leadership means staying true to your values and leading with a walk and talk that is consistent. This walk and talk means being true and genuine and becoming a leader who leads through integrity. Something that is not a mask but a reflection of who one is.

Authentic leadership: Staying true to your values and leading with integrity starts by knowing who you are and what is of value.

If you want to be that person of influence who thrives through moments requiring more than resilience, I would be honored to be part of the team supporting that journey. This is not a program to take, but the process of commitment to growing forward.

This is not a solo effort. Life may not be a team sport, but success is never an individual accomplishment.

I love being in the boat with real people in those critical moments because once they are through the storm, we get to see their passion and purpose come to life. That is an amazing point when you decide to not settle for being "fine," or "good." When being real becomes the reality, it automatically inspires others to an authenticity and integrity.

Let's have that conversation about being the authentic leadership that people so desperately want. Staying true to your values and leading with integrity means we all thrive.

About the Author

To thrive through critical moments, be it a crisis, change or growth, is to have more than a plan, procedure, or a policy, but an active, enthusiastic practise. Leveraging the principles of muscle-memory to enable leadership, people, and organizations thrive [not merely settle for resilience], means it must be a way-of-being not a task on a to-do list.

John R. Robertson, founder and President of FORTLOG Services Inc., an established and trusted company with over 30 years in transforming critical moments in a variety of contexts. Strengthening leadership which people can trust and want to follow develops a culture where people want to work.

John provides the values-anchored approach for his clients to create purposeful, productive, ways to accomplish things. Integrating social intelligence thinking so motives and relationships enable people to fit in and flourish. Encouraging groups to get things done, and maintain good relationships with one another, fosters true strength through critical moments.

Inspired and driven by his values, John acts as a facilitator for his clients as they test, discover, and expand what they can do. He uses concrete, verifiable processes to help them achieve demonstrable, solution-focused results. Remaining faithful to his passion and values,

John invests himself in his vocation without reservation. He provides spirit-filled, insightful guidance that his clients use to amplify their lives and their businesses. John truly provides "leadership that people can follow through storms."

This is achieved through the values-anchored Run towards the Roar Ethos, after all, *BUSINESS WORKS WHEN PEOPLE THRIVE!*

Connect with John

LinkedIn: https://www.linkedin.com/in/johnrobertson-fortlog/

Website: www.fortlog.co

A Simple Framework for Women Leaders to Adapt to Change and Find Opportunity in Adversity

By Adela Vladutoiu

For my grandfather, my role model and my hero!

Life has shown me that change is inevitable. Sometimes, it arrives smoothly, bringing joy and ease. Yet, more often, change brings discomfort and challenges. Just when you think you've overcome one obstacle and you are close to your goal, another appears, testing your resolve once more.

Reflecting on my unexpected journey, I'm amazed by the many changes in my life, starting from my early years. Born in communist Romania, I was raised in a small village in the southern part of the country. My family was middle class. While my parents were the first generation not working the land –definitely not wealthy—they provided me with something far more valuable than material possessions: a strong sense of values and respect. During my final year of high school, in December 1989, Romania underwent a dramatic transformation. The revolution that swept through the country brought an end to the communist system, but it also led to the collapse of the economy. I became the first in my family to attend university, pursuing a degree in engineering, but by the time I graduated, finding work as an engineer in the broken industry had become very challenging. Fortunately, I secured a position with a starting private company in the construction industry, and although the experience was demanding, it only served to reinforce my work ethic and resilience. Nine years later, as Romania continued to evolve, I transitioned to the corporate world, joining one of the global leaders in agri-business that was just entering the Romanian market. I became part of their post-merger team following an acquisition and then started to rise through the ranks until I became the first female Plant Manager and, finally, General Manager.

My career journey continued to evolve. After spending 11 years in agribusiness, I transitioned to the packaging industry, working for international companies, where I held positions as Managing Director and Board Member. Finally, in 2023, I took a significant step by deciding to pursue my passions and embark on my own projects and business venture.

Throughout these years of change and the inevitable challenges that accompanied my career growth, I strived to live by the principles I learned at home, particularly from my grandfather. My grandfather, a World War II veteran, remains my role model and hero. Upon returning home after the war, he found a country already in the grip of the communist regime, with him and our family treated as "enemies of the state." Despite these hardships, he lived by the very principle he also taught me: always with dignity. One of my most vivid childhood memories is of a bitter winter day when I was trudging home from school in a blizzard, with my head down. My grandfather stood in the middle of the road, waiting for me and looking at me intently. On that day, he imparted a lesson that has guided me ever since: "Regardless of what happens to you or around you, always keep your head up."

This mantra has been my guiding light as I've navigated a career that's taken me from humble beginnings to C-level roles in traditionally male-dominated industries. Along this journey, I've learned that success isn't about adhering to complex theories or rigid goals. Instead, it's about developing a flexible mindset and effective systems that create a sustainable path forward while smartly navigating the obstacles placed your way.

As I consider the multitude of changes and challenges I've faced, I'm reminded of the power of resilience and adaptability. I did not always get it right, I made mistakes and wrong choices, but I never lost myself. But to achieve this, you must learn to concentrate on what truly matters and resist outside noise, no matter how overwhelming it may be. There's a Romanian proverb about "separating wheat from chaffs," which perfectly illustrates what we should do in life: discern the essential from the trivial. This approach enabled me to face changes effectively and find opportunities in life challenges, my sole wish is to have understood it earlier.

What follows is a simple yet powerful framework for embracing change, overcoming adversity, and thriving in leadership roles, especially for women. Drawing from my personal experiences, I'll share insights on how to adapt, persevere, and master the art of separating the wheat from the chaff in your own life. Throughout these pages, you'll gain:

1. Strategies for embracing your true self and overcoming the 'Good Girl Syndrome.'

2. Techniques for recognizing and addressing workplace biases.

3. Tools for effectively managing challenging personalities.

4. Methods for building and maintaining healthy boundaries to prevent burnout.

5. Empowering approaches to self-advocacy and breaking the glass ceiling.

Whether you're at the start of your career or a seasoned leader looking to refine your approach, this chapter offers practical, actionable insights to elevate your leadership and empower both yourself and those around you. Consider this the **ABCDE of women's leadership—the fundamental principles that form the bedrock of success**. By internalizing these core concepts, you'll build a solid foundation for enduring success and fulfillment in your leadership journey.

Join me as we explore how to thrive in this ever-changing world of leadership, always keeping our heads up, just as my grandfather taught me.

A. Embracing <u>Authenticity</u>

As we embark on this journey together, let's start with the cornerstone of exceptional leadership: authenticity. While this term is often overused, I cannot overstate its importance. I remember when, many years ago, a younger colleague who knew me from home was surprised by how differently I behaved in the office compared to my true self. At times, I felt compelled to wear a 'mask,' believing it would help me integrate, gain acceptance, meet expectations, and perform better. However, I realised this approach was misguided. Real strength doesn't come from adapting to others' expectations—you will never be able to meet them all—but from embracing your true self.

The Power of Being Yourself

Throughout my career in male-dominated industries, I encountered the pervasive notion that success for women meant adopting stereotypically male characteristics. I was told that women were too emotional, lacked confidence compared to men, and needed to "toughen up" to succeed. Naturally, this counsel was deemed equally applicable to me, as though my gender would predetermine my professional shortcomings.

Initially, I felt pressured to adopt a more aggressive or competitive demeanour to fit in. However, this only led to unnecessary conflicts, internal struggles, and a sense of inauthenticity. But here's the truth: Through experience, I realized that embracing who I really was unlocked unique strengths that were equally, if not more valuable, than those typically associated with male leadership. My empathy allowed me to forge deeper connections with colleagues. My emotional intelligence helped me navigate complex situations, and my intuition guided effective decision-making.

Embracing authenticity wasn't easy. It required acknowledging and accepting my weaknesses and even the potential downsides of my strengths—a vulnerable and often uncomfortable process. However, when we women leaders unapologetically embrace our true selves, we inspire others to do the same. By being authentic, we build genuine connections, create trust, and give rise to a more supportive work culture for everyone.

Overcoming the Good Girl Syndrome

The journey towards authenticity often requires challenging deeply ingrained societal expectations. One of the most pervasive is the 'Good Girl Syndrome'—a set of unwritten rules that can significantly hinder our growth and potential as leaders.

As women, we face societal pressure to be polite, agreeable, and non-confrontational. We're often indirectly told to keep quiet, not rock the boat, or express opinions that differ from others. In my career, I faced situations where I was advised to be a good girl, stay quiet, and not cause disruptions.

And, through experiencing it, I realised that the Good Girl Syndrome is more than just a set of behavioural expectations; it's a psychological trap that can have far-reaching consequences. It creates a constant internal struggle as we deal with the tension between societal norms and our own ambitions and authentic selves. It's a silent saboteur, undermining our confidence and limiting our potential.

Breaking free from this syndrome is no small feat. It requires conscious effort, unwavering determination, and a willingness to challenge not just others' expectations but also our own internalised beliefs. Here are some strategies I've found effective in overcoming the Good Girl Syndrome:

1. **Be Assertive.** Assertiveness is not about being aggressive; it's the art of expressing your thoughts, needs, and boundaries clearly and confidently. Practice using "I" statements to convey your perspective. For example, instead of saying, "Maybe we could consider..." try, "I believe we should..." This subtle shift can greatly influence how your ideas are received.

2. **Embrace Constructive Conflict.** Recognize that disagreement can lead to better outcomes. Learn to see disagreements not as personal attacks but as opportunities to explore different viewpoints and arrive at better solutions. Engage in healthy debate and encourage others to do the same. Remember, a team that never disagrees is likely missing out on valuable insights.

3. **Challenge Perfectionism.** As women, we often feel immense pressure to get everything right, constantly second-guessing ourselves and agonizing over minor details. But the truth is, perfectionism is not your ally; it's a formidable foe that can lead to procrastination, anxiety, and burnout. Instead, prioritize progress and continuous improvement. Celebrate your achievements, learn from your mistakes, and remember that imperfection is human.

4. **Develop a Growth Mindset.** Rather than perceiving challenges as threats to your abilities, regard them as opportunities for learning and growth. When confronted with a tough task, instead of doubting your competence by thinking, "I'm not good enough for this," adopt the mindset of, "This is an opportunity to develop and enhance my skills." This shift in perspective can be transformative, turning obstacles into stepping stones for your personal and professional growth.

As we assert ourselves more confidently, we often encounter a new set of challenges: the biases and labels that others may try to impose upon us. In the next section, we'll explore strategies for navigating these obstacles while staying true to our authentic selves.

41

B. Navigating <u>Biases</u> and Labels

As a woman leader, navigating the professional world can feel like walking through a minefield. Every move is scrutinized through the lens of gender-based societal expectations. If you're assertive or decisive, you risk being labelled as aggressive or unfeminine. Conversely, showing empathy and cooperation might lead others to perceive you as weak or lacking leadership qualities. The weight of these conflicting expectations can be overwhelming, causing many talented women to second-guess their every move or, worse, to dim their light to fit into a mold that was never designed for them. But it's crucial to remember that these biases, though persistent, are not insurmountable. By acknowledging their existence and actively working to challenge them, we can begin to reshape the narrative around women in leadership.

Understanding the Double-Bind Dilemma

The bias described above is known as the 'Double-Bind Dilemma,' which significantly contributes to the challenges women face in leadership roles and can severely impede their career advancement. It underscores the persistent gender stereotypes and biases prevalent in many professional environments, specifically highlighting the contradictory expectations women leaders encounter in the work-place. This creates a "damned if you do, damned if you don't" scenario, where women feel trapped between conflicting societal expectations and must navigate a narrow path between being "too soft" and "too tough," often facing criticism or negative perceptions regardless of the approach they take. A clear example is when a woman's behaviour as a leader is deemed unacceptable, while the same behaviour in a male leader is seen as a sign of strength and success.

While the double-bind presents a significant challenge, it's not insurmountable. Recognizing its existence is the first step; without this awareness, you may find yourself trapped in a cycle of frustration and dissatisfaction. The next step is to develop effective strategies to navigate and ultimately overcome it.

As I've progressed in my career, I've discovered that success lies not in making yourself small to please others but in skillfully moving forward. These strategies aren't about changing who you are to fit into a biased system. Rather, they're about empowering yourself to challenge that system while staying true to your authentic self. By mastering these techniques, we can turn the double-bind dilemma from a roadblock into a stepping stone for your leadership journey.

Strategies to Overcome Bias

1. **Challenge Stereotypes Proactively:** Have the courage to address bias whenever you encounter it. This may involve engaging in challenging discussions with colleagues or superiors and persistently advocating for changes within your organization. It also necessitates self-awareness and dedication to confronting your own internalized limiting beliefs. Regularly reflect on your own thoughts and behaviours to identify and eliminate negative self-talk. Remember, change begins from within.

2. **Seek Support from Mentors and Allies:** Build a strong, diverse support network. This could include peer support groups, professional associations for women, or even online communities. Mentors are invaluable, providing both practical guidance and emotional support drawn from their own

experiences. Allies within the organization can be powerful advocates for change, aiding in the dismantling of systemic barriers. Seek out multiple mentors and allies—both within and outside your organization—to gain diverse perspectives.

3. **Balance Assertiveness With Likability:** This means developing a communication style that is both confident and approachable. Practice using "confident language" by removing qualifiers like "just," "maybe," or "sorry" from your speech. Use strong, declarative statements while maintaining an open and collaborative tone. Develop the ability to read the room and adapt your communication style as needed. This flexibility helps you navigate various situations.

4. **Embrace a Resilient Mindset:** Finally, see challenges not as insurmountable obstacles but as opportunities for personal growth and development. Recognize that encountering biases does not reflect your worth or abilities. When faced with bias, ask yourself, "What can I learn from this situation?" and "How can I use this experience to become stronger?" Reframe biases as opportunities to acquire new skills, develop innovative strategies, and ground yourself in your achievements instead of focusing on the negative.

As you navigate biases and labels, you'll find that your newfound confidence and authenticity will be tested in various situations. One of the most challenging aspects of leadership is dealing with difficult personalities. In the next section, we'll explore how to handle these encounters in a way that not only preserves your integrity but also turns potential conflicts into opportunities for growth and positive change.

C. Dealing with Challenging People

Imagine this scenario: you're leading a team meeting, and one or more colleagues are consistently uncooperative, frequently interrupting you and others, and treating the meeting as a stage for their own agenda. You might be tempted to remain silent, avoiding the elephant in the room to keep the peace. However, this approach is ineffective and will ultimately fail. Remaining passive in the face of such behaviour doesn't just fail to resolve the issue; it actively undermines your position and erodes your reputation. Ignoring obvious problems sends a message of weakness, indecision, or worse, indifference.

The lesson here is clear: Addressing difficult personalities and behaviours promptly and directly is not just advisable but essential for maintaining your own leadership credibility. It may be uncomfortable in the moment, but the long-term benefits far outweigh the temporary discomfort of confrontation.

Recognizing and Addressing Challenging Behaviours

Navigating challenging personalities is an unavoidable aspect of any professional environment, yet it can be particularly daunting for women leaders already facing biases and preconceived notions. Whether it's colleagues or managers with conflicting priorities, or demanding clients with unrealistic expectations, these interactions can create a tense and difficult atmosphere. As a woman leader, I have discovered the importance of keenly identifying such behaviours early and addressing them proactively to maintain a productive workspace.

Difficult behaviours can manifest in many forms, from outright aggression to subtle, passive-aggressive remarks or uncooperative attitudes. The first step in managing these individuals effectively is to recognize their behaviours and understand their impact on you, the team, and the overall work environment. It's important to acknowledge that every team and organization will have such individuals; thinking otherwise is unrealistic. Identifying these signs requires a blend of emotional intelligence and self-awareness and must be followed by decisive action to address these issues directly.

I've learned that avoiding or postponing difficult conversations often leads to frustration and defensiveness. The key takeaway is to engage in these conversations promptly. Choose the time and place thoughtfully, with clear purpose and intention, but make sure to initiate the discussion before someone else does. This might involve having a direct conversation with the individual, discussing the repercussions of their actions, and finding ways to improve the situation.

Approach these conversations with empathy and an open mind, ensuring that you set clear expectations and establish well-defined agreements. This strategy not only helps alleviate tensions and promote transparency but also establishes crucial professional boundaries.

Emotional Intelligence and Effective Communication

Throughout my career, I've learned that communication is not just about what we say but how we say it. I recall a particularly tense meeting where a colleague was persistently difficult. Initially, I responded with frustration rather than taking a deep breath and tapping into my emotional intelligence. The next time, however, I avoided making the same mistake. By understanding and managing my own emotions, while also recognizing and influencing the emotions of others, I was able to transform a potential confrontation into a constructive dialogue. This experience taught me that emotional intelligence isn't just a buzzword—it's a crucial skill for navigating the complex interpersonal dynamics of leadership.

As you climb the professional ladder, taking on greater responsibilities and navigating more complex interpersonal dynamics, challenging situations don't decrease—they multiply. The higher the position, the higher the stakes, and the more frequent and intense these interpersonal challenges become. As women leaders, we possess a unique strength in emotional intelligence, an essential skill for managing conflicts and difficult individuals. With a keen understanding of empathy and effective communication, we can cultivate strong relationships and foster a collaborative, supportive work environment.

Here are some tools for leveraging emotional intelligence and effective communication:

1. **Focus on the Behaviour Rather Than Assigning Blame.** Utilize "I" statements; instead of saying, "You always miss deadlines," try "I feel frustrated when deadlines are missed." This shifts the narrative from personal to facts.

2. **Practice Active Listening.** Give your full attention to the speaker, acknowledge their perspective, and ask clarifying questions to ensure understanding.

3. **Seek to Understand.** Try to uncover the root cause of difficult behaviour. Often, there are underlying issues or concerns driving the behaviour.

4. **Set Clear Expectations.** Communicate your expectations clearly and provide specific feedback when those expectations aren't met.

5. **Manage Your Own Emotions.** Recognize your emotional triggers and develop strategies for staying calm and composed in challenging situations.

6. **Choose Your Battles.** Not every difficult interaction requires a confrontation. Learn to discern which issues are worth addressing and which can be let go.

As you sharpen your skills in managing challenging personalities, remember that it's equally important to recognize when these interactions begin to take a toll on your well-being. This brings us to another vital aspect of leadership: developing and maintaining healthy boundaries. In the next section, we'll explore how to create balance while navigating the demands of leadership.

D. <u>Developing</u> Healthy Boundaries

Many of us find ourselves caught in a cycle of overwork—staying late at the office, being the last to leave, bringing work home into family time, on holidays, and even on sick days. We continuously push our own limits without questioning this status quo. But we must ask ourselves: How sustainable is this behaviour, and how long until it leads to burnout and failure? I've learned this lesson the hard way— twice. My first encounter with burnout came during the initial decade of my career when I was eager to prove myself. The second time, years later, when I should have known better. Yet, I fell into the same trap, which illustrates how subtle and difficult this cycle is to break.

There's a misguided pride in our constant availability and unwavering dedication, where we confuse exhaustion with responsibility and equate our worth with our willingness to sacrifice everything for work. This mindset is especially dangerous for women, who often feel the need to work twice as hard as their male counterparts to gain equal recognition. This toxic combination—the pressure to overperform, the internalized belief that we must always be "on," and the gender-based expectation of extra effort—creates a perfect storm. It's a recipe for burnout that disproportionately affects women, leading many to leave their roles earlier than their male peers after depleting all their energy reserves.

The Importance of Self-Care

Self-care encompasses both physical and emotional health. In a professional setting, this means taking steps to manage stress levels, maintain a sustainable workload, and prioritize personal well-being. This can be especially challenging in high-pressure environments where job demands can feel overwhelming.

To me, the key aspect of self-care is setting clear and healthy boundaries. This not only involves specifying what is acceptable in terms of workload and working hours but also setting limits for interpersonal interactions and engagements. It means being brave enough to say NO to unreasonable requests that could ultimately harm your well-being. By establishing these boundaries and sticking to them, we are actively choosing to put our health first, and that is something worth prioritizing. I understand well that establishing boundaries is challenging, especially if you haven't done so before. Often, you will encounter negative reactions from others, which can discourage you. You might feel tempted to be inconsistent or even give up, as breaking habits requires effort. However, it's the results that matter, so keep pushing forward.

Strategies for Creating Balance

First, let me be honest: I don't believe a perfect work-life balance is attainable. There will always be times when one aspect of your life takes precedence over another. However, I do believe that balance within imbalance is possible through acknowledgment, self-awareness, and thoughtful, practical methods.

1. **Prioritize**: Identifying the most critical areas in your life requires more than a simple to-do list. It necessitates a deep dive into your personal values, long-term goals, and what genuinely brings you fulfilment. Begin by conducting a comprehensive life audit. Evaluate each aspect of your life, rating your satisfaction and the importance of each. This exercise will highlight areas needing more attention and those that may be consuming too much of your energy. Once you've pinpointed your priorities, channel your energy into activities that align with your core values and long-term objectives.

2. **Delegate**: Delegating responsibilities is essential for preventing burnout and enhancing productivity. Despite societal pressures to shoulder multiple burdens, leaders must recognize that we cannot manage everything alone. By entrusting tasks to team members, you not only alleviate your stress but also

provide opportunities for others to develop their skills and grow professionally.

3. **Learn to say 'No':** Mastering the art of strategically saying no is crucial for preserving your mental and physical health. This involves declining requests or opportunities that don't align with your priorities or jeopardize your well-being. It also requires setting realistic expectations for yourself and others to maintain a balanced and fulfilling lifestyle. Remember, saying no to one thing allows you to say yes to something that better aligns with your priorities.

4. **Conduct Regular Life Audits:** Schedule regular life audit sessions to evaluate your overall well-being and progress toward your goals. Reflect on what's working well and pinpoint areas needing improvement. Be honest with yourself about whether your current lifestyle aligns with your values and long-term aspirations. Based on these evaluations, make necessary adjustments to your routines, commitments, and goals. Remember, achieving balance is a continuous process, not a final destination.

As we move forward, we'll explore how to channel this newfound balance into breaking through the glass ceiling and inspiring others. In the next section, we will explore strategies for empowering yourself and advocating for your success despite systemic challenges.

E. Empowering Yourself

I've observed that men often overestimate their capabilities and achievements, while women tend to undervalue theirs. There's a noticeable gender disparity in self-promotion, with men rating their performance more favourably than women who perform equally well. The common thread here for women is self-doubt, with many uncertain about their actual level of performance.

I can still recall important key moments, particularly my first high-stakes meeting as a newly appointed General Manager and my inaugural Board presentation. After delivering my carefully prepared and rehearsed remarks, I felt a noticeable shift in the room—initial scepticism gave way to attentiveness and, perhaps, a glimmer of respect. I had meticulously prepared, knowing that thorough ground-work is essential for success. Yet, as I stood there, I realized that one crucial element was vital in fully winning over the room: banishing my self-doubt.

This experience taught me a valuable lesson. While preparation and knowledge are vital, they alone are not enough. The final, critical ingredient is an unshakeable belief in yourself. It's about silencing that inner voice of doubt and standing firm in your capabilities and vision.

Self-Advocacy and Confidence

Championing oneself is indispensable for women striving to excel in leadership positions. It encompasses the active promotion of personal achievements, the assertive articulation of your viewpoints, and an unwavering belief in your own capabilities.

Self-advocacy is not bragging; it is far from it! It is taking proactive control of your professional journey and ensuring that your con-tributions are recognized and valued. This means vocally celebrating your accomplishments, relentlessly seeking out opportunities for growth, and standing firm in the pursuit of equitable treatment and advancement.

A pivotal element of self-advocacy is conquering impostor syndrome, that persistent feeling of inadequacy and fear of being exposed as lacking, despite clear evidence of success. It continually amazes me how many successful and accomplished women still struggle with this issue. While I won't dive into the reasons behind it now, effectively combating impostor syndrome starts with recognizing it and then taking immediate action to stop it. Here are some simple yet essential steps:

1. Acknowledge and enjoy your achievements.

2. Solicit constructive feedback and support from trusted colleagues.

3. Actively challenge any negative self-perceptions that may arise.

4. Reframe self-doubt as a sign of growth and learning, not inadequacy.

Breaking the Glass Ceiling

Many women have encountered the glass ceiling in their professional lives. It is not just a metaphor but an invisible barrier reinforced by prejudices, stereotypes, and organizational cultures steeped in male favouritism.

In my journey, I've had my fair share of encounters with this metaphorical barrier. I remember the first time I truly felt its presence—I was qualified and had proven my worth time and again, yet I watched a less experienced male colleague promoted ahead of me. It was a stark reminder that self-advocacy and confidence, while essential, are just the beginning. We need both to break through the glass ceiling, but we need even more than that: a clear and effective approach that we take ownership of without any false humility.

1. **Embrace Disobedience:** Cultivate an unyielding rebellion against the restrictive norms that confine women's ambitions. Find out for yourself how you can challenge it in your organization and what transformative changes you could advocate for. This could manifest as denouncing unjust practices, advocating for policy changes, or daringly taking new paths.

2. **Harness Unique Perspectives:** Be bold in using your unique insights as tools for achieving progress and innovation. Think about what experiences and insights you bring to the table and how you can leverage these assets to drive innovation and progress. Your distinct perspectives and experiences are not weaknesses to be hidden but powerful assets to be leveraged.

3. **Master the Art of Negotiation:** Women often face unique challenges in negotiations, from salary discussions to project assignments. Don't shy away from asking whether it's a promotion, a raise, or a high-profile project. Think about how you can enhance your negotiation skills, backed by confidence in your worth, and what you need to be able to confidently ask for what you deserve.

4. **Cultivate Visibility:** Make your achievements known. Strategize how you can increase your visibility in and outside your organization. Be smartly loud, volunteer for high-profile

projects, speak up in meetings, and ensure your contributions are recognized. Know that invisibility is the enemy of advancement.

As you enjoy your hard-earned success, realize this is more than a personal triumph—it's a testament to the power of authentic leadership in breaking down barriers. Your journey has brought you to this point, but it's only the beginning. In what follows, we'll reflect on how these strategies create a robust framework for your unique leadership style and how you can continue to grow and inspire others throughout your leadership journey.

Embrace Your Own Leadership Journey

At the end of this exploration of adapting to change and finding opportunity in adversity, let's reflect on the key themes that form the foundation of resilient, authentic leadership. Your journey, like mine, is unique and filled with its own challenges and triumphs. Yet, the lessons we've discussed are universal, empowering you to not just survive but thrive in the ever-changing landscape of leadership where each obstacle overcome is a step toward empowering not just yourself but all women in leadership.

Embracing our own journey is more than a buzzword; it's the cornerstone of impactful leadership. By shedding the masks we often wear to fit in, we unlock our full potential and create space for others to do the same. Our unique perspectives and experiences are not weaknesses to be hidden but powerful assets to be leveraged.

As you move forward, consider these action steps to continue your growth:

1. Regularly reassess yourself. Are you leading in a way that aligns with your true self? Remember, authenticity is a strength, not a weakness in leadership.

2. Identify one specific way you can apply each strategy in your current role or situation.

3. Celebrate your successes, no matter how small, and use them to build your confidence.

4. Practice self-compassion; be kind to yourself. Recognize that change takes time and that setbacks are part of the process, and treat yourself with the same compassion and understanding you would offer a close friend.

5. Seek out opportunities to mentor other women, passing on the lessons you've learned.

The journey of leadership is not a straight path. It's filled with twists, turns, and sometimes, unexpected detours. But with each challenge you face and overcome, you grow stronger and wiser. Your experiences—both triumphs and setbacks—shape you into the leader you are meant to be.

As you continue on your path, carry with you the words of my grandfather: "Always keep your head up." Let this be your mantra as you face new challenges and seize new opportunities.

About the Author – Adela Vladutoiu

Adela Vladutoiu is a trailblazer in the business world, known for breaking glass ceilings and building bridges.

With nearly three decades as a Senior Executive Leader, she has shattered barriers in the manufacturing and consumer goods sectors, working for industry giants such as Cargill, Bunge, and Greiner, in traditionally male-dominated fields and international environments. Adela has held pivotal leadership positions, including being the first woman Plant Director and General Manager for some companies, as well as serving as Country Managing Director, Board Director, and Board President.

Adding entrepreneurship to her extensive corporate leadership experience, Adela now provides strategic and operational support for small and medium-sized businesses focused on long-term growth. Her passion lies in championing women in leadership through professional and business mentorship, equipping them with tools to navigate workplace challenges and advance their careers.

Adela's commitment to continuous learning is evident in her Executive MBA from Tiffin University and her ongoing pursuit of a Doctorate in Business Administration, embedding her two areas of interest: supporting women in leadership and building sustainable businesses.

In addition to her native Romanian, Adela speaks English and French and has a lifelong passion for reading and a curiosity for knowledge, born from her years growing up. Describing herself as a 'pragmatic dreamer,' Adela believes in balancing governance and profit with personal fulfillment. She often says, "The P&L of life is as important as any business metric. We all have the right to pursue our passions and live by our own values."

Through her mentorship, consultancy, and advocacy, Adela is dedicated to sharing her hard-won insights. Her mission is to shape a new generation of leaders who can effectively balance pragmatism with vision and professional success with personal satisfaction.

Connect with Adela

www.LinkedIn.com/in/Adela-Vladutoiu

www.LinkedIn.com/company/ThinkAheadAdvisory/

Email: thinkaheadadvisory@outlook.com

Resilience Habits
From the Inside Out

By Emily Marquis

I woke up, again, at three in the morning, crippled with stress, worry, anger, unhappiness, and guilt. My mind was running a mile a minute, just in time for shame to enter. Insomnia had become a familiar norm in my life that seemed to bring his unwanted friend exhaustion and irritability alongside regular stomach pains and digestive issues that I didn't have time for. I was raising two toddlers, running a successful consulting business with a staff, living in my dream home, having a community with friends, and having a typical marriage. All at the same time, everything felt wrong. I wanted to jump out of my skin.

Resistant to the array of pills doctors were too quick to prescribe for unexplainable symptoms, my life consisted of having a glass of wine, working as hard as I could to provide, and surviving the day of pulling expectations while trying to be the best mom, wife, and friend, I could be. It was no longer working, and I couldn't kid myself anymore. The whispers I'd heard from my body, mind, and emotions turned into yells that were hitting me with two by fours of chronic conditions, burnout, relationship challenges, and stark unhappiness and overwhelm.

A much deeper story had built into my cells and neurological patterns that shouted to be heard each time I looked into my daughter's beautiful, innocent eyes. My culminating past and shaky present were eating me up from the inside out, and it was time to peel back the layers of my life's onion and save my future. If not for my daughters to have the best mom they could be, then finally, for me.

Over the next several years, I made a solid commitment to shine a light on my deeper-rooted challenges one by one. Not all at once, but intentionally, slowly, over time when I felt ready; I started a mindfulness practice of my own liking, went to individual therapy, went to couple's therapy, changed my diet, exercised more, spent more time in nature, built friendships that aligned with who I indeed was and wanted to become, reduced my alcohol and substances, adhered to necessary medications, tackled chronic conditions and prioritized sleep. After figuring out who I was and where I wanted to go, I created micro habits that aligned with my values. My typical days grew into routines that defined my path. I learned how to be a real parent and truly understand what it means to be nice to myself from the inside out. Over time, this also meant significant changes on the outside; moving, divorcing, choosing to have no contact with my biological family, and changing careers. While this can feel extreme and is not the necessary path for everyone, I knew that with my new way of life, the foundation needed to be built to support it.

Before, I thought mistakes and unexpected adverse outcomes were valid reasons to imprison myself into days of self-criticism. I am incredibly human and imperfect. Now, I continue to make mistakes like everyone else, which I recognize as everyday life and learning, not a detour from it. I can take them in my stride and handle them with pride. Or, if I can't handle them alone, I have the right people and tools to ask for help, meaning the storm only lasts for a short time. This is what resilience feels like in my cells, heart, and soul. On the outside, I have probably always looked put together and lived a "normal" life. Now, I share more authentic challenges and show up unapologetically to a workout class without having time to brush my teeth. I dedicate my life to helping people build resilience tools to deal with their crises or everyday life ripples, whether they show up inside or outside our bodies. Sometimes, we have to make significant changes if the yells are coming. Still, we are lucky enough to hear or prevent even the whispers. In that case, we can make slow, manageable micro changes over time. If I can do it, anyone can, and you don't have to do it alone. The relief and empowerment that comes from seeking help and making changes is a beacon of hope, guiding us toward a brighter future.

In my formal education and life experiences, I have discovered nine specific ways to take small steps over time that we will form into habits and rituals that will formulate who we truly are. These will be our ingredients for resilience and help us feel well from the inside out. How we spend our time reflects our values and vision of ourselves. Sometimes, the foundation must be broken or rebuilt, and no one has to do it alone. Let's let go of perfection and take one small step toward change at a time together.

Self-Understanding. Awareness is our superpower. As we pause to zoom out, we zoom in to look at the patterns in many aspects of our lives. We need awareness and understanding to know where to begin making edits or nurturing habits we love. Inspire yourself with a growth mindset, which means that change is possible, feedback is helpful, and mistakes are the best detours. Commit to whatever practices help create awareness for you. This could be journaling, meditation, or seeking feedback from trusted friends or mentors. Commitment to doing something is, in itself, a giant first step toward awareness. As you do this, you'll begin to notice. Notice your body, behaviors, thinking, strengths, values, patterns, communication, relationships, what you like, what's not working, and where your growth edge can be. Look at those whispers in all areas of your life, one at a time, before they turn into yells or the devastating two-by-four. Once we notice our patterns and get data on our bodies, we also get to love ourselves and create habits and tools that make us feel good. We can be our biggest cheerleader. At first, talking kindly to myself felt strange and a little cheesy. Now, I am my biggest supporter and listen to voices that tell me when to cool it. It is a beautiful dialogue that I'm proud of. Once we truly know who we are, we can create habits and rituals that fuel us, not suppress us. Tools such as self-compassion, value alignment for decision-making, boundaries, gratitude, health habits, and grace become strong voices of abundant beckoning and ease sets in. Remember, self-compassion and self-care are not indulgences but necessities that make us feel valued and encouraged to prioritize our well-being.

What signs of discontentment in your life have you been ignoring?

What daily patterns and behaviors serve your values?

What makes you uniquely, unapologetically you?

Healthcare Adherence. Fortunately, we don't have to cultivate awareness and sort through what we find on our own. Plenty of people out there can help us if we allow them to. Seeking help in any area is not a weakness. Therapists are outstanding professionals who help us draw awareness to challenges from our past that create patterns in our present and offer tools to release or work with them. It's incredibly courageous and liberating. I have celebrated being in therapy for over twelve years. While I may not be in "crisis mode," one of my tools is having a space to sort things out emotionally and mentally, stay on track, and receive much-needed feedback. We also want to get a pulse on what's happening in our bodies. Visit your doctor of choice; a primary biomedical doctor, a specialist, a functional medicine doctor, a naturopath, a dentist, a nutritionist, or even a shaman. With more data, we can support ourselves instead of feeling poorly, wondering, or worrying. So often, we may tolerate fear, pain, or dysfunction in our physical body. We deserve to feel well, starting with a baseline of knowledge. Then, we can create tools for adhering to plans we co-create with our providers, whether taking medication, supplements, follow-up exams, or more. The relief from seeking professional help is immense and a crucial part of our wellness journey.

What does your healthcare support team look like?

How do you stay on track?

Sleep. Most people aren't experiencing the quality or quantity of sleep they need, and many factors and patterns play into that. Very few species on this planet are not created to have a sleeping pattern—it's a must for survival. Everything rolls off our shoulders or becomes clearer after a good night's rest. And yet, it can seem like the world is against us for setting ourselves up for sleep. To create a beautiful wind-down ritual, make a comfy space, work to ease your mind, and give yourself time to sleep. If you still can't sleep, it might be a secondary factor, meaning it's time to seek help on the root cause. Prioritizing sleep supports our overall well-being.

When do you feel fully rested?

What sets you up for a successful quality night of sleep?

Stress. Life does not exist without aging or stress; there is no anti-aging or anti-stress—sorry! But remember, we are each built to be able to respond to stress. The challenge is that we may not have coping skills, so we stay in our stress response or allow too many stressors into our lives simultaneously, derailing resilience. First, we look at our relationship with stress; is it something to fear or resist? Or is it something that is natural and can be handled? Do the cons of your stressors outweigh or get balanced out by their pros? Take time to zoom out and look at your relationship with stress, and identify the stressors in your life. Are there any that can go? Is there anything that you can be more tolerant of? Then, take a look at what your stress-coping skills are that are nourishing. Options might be mindfulness, meditation, breathing, somatic exercises, physical exercise, talking with a supportive person, journaling, dancing, listening to music, yelling and crying, resting, positive self-talk, or more. Remember, stress is inevitable, but how we relate to and roll through it are the tools that will determine our future. You have the power to choose your tools.

What is your relationship to stress?

What tools make you feel most relaxed and resilient?

Healthy Eating. What we put into our bodies reflects our values and nourishment. Unfortunately, healthy eating and drinking are also tied to many patterns attached to emotional baggage, fundamental social determinants of health, and societal influences. Perfection is not the goal. When our body feels well and is appropriately fueled, it is the most significant tool to help us approach life. It takes time to know current patterns, where they are coming from, and where we'd like to go to feel well. We can start by having less sugar, less alcohol, less takeout, and a little more fruits, veggies, water, and simple home-cooked meals. The importance of healthy eating cannot be overstated. It's a key component of our well-being; by committing to it, we can feel motivated and positive about our overall health.

What's your favorite healthy meal that makes you feel full?

What eating habit is no longer serving you?

Movement. The way we take care of our body is a metaphor for how we show up in the world. When we move our body with flow, joy, and creativity, we engage in energetic exertion, address stressors of resistance, and embrace ease, stretch, and personal touch. We now live in a generally sedentary world where we have to intentionally fit in movement. Or, to the other extreme, we must fit in rest and stretching. It's important to notice our balance. Both moving and resting are important to prepare our body to handle the many things life throws our way.

What type of movement do you most enjoy?

How can you sneak in small movements throughout the day?

Creativity and Play. I don't know about you, but as I age, life becomes more severe and responsible. Joy, play, passion, and creativity take the backseat to my carefully laid structure to make life work. This can be when we think we have lost a part of ourselves. Or are you doing playful things that no longer fit into who you want to be? Remember what your passions are and what makes you laugh. Try to do it once in a while and loosen it up. Reignite who you already are.

What is your creative outlet or hobby?

What passion did you enjoy most as a child?

Relationships and Support. Whether we are 7 or 70, building new relationships with friends, family, work colleagues, or other members of our community is vulnerable and humbling. It's essential to have at least one or two meaningful relationships and be surrounded by several at a like-minded community event. Even with much effort, not all relationships are forever. We all grow, or don't, and become unmatched. All of our relationships and how we relate to them are a choice. It's vital that healthy, supportive relationships, even if only one or two, are the ones that take up the most mental time in real estate in our lives. By 'mental real estate,' I mean the time and energy we invest to consider and maintain these relationships. Does this mean we quit every other relationship? That's up to you. Or we could give non-healthy relationships like an annoying co-worker or clingy in-law less mental real estate and focus on building, strengthening, and thinking about relationships with those who will have our back in our darkest times and laugh at our worst jokes unconditionally. And it won't feel like an obligation when you reciprocate.

Who is on your star support team?

Who does or doesn't align with who you want to become?

Environment. Our external environment has a significant impact on us externally and internally. Our home, car, office, neighborhood, schedule, information intake, visuals, noise, smells, and earth are all included. It's about what we surround ourselves with and how we care for it. Sometimes, not everything is in our control. There is usually something we can do—add some color, remove clutter, move furniture around, buy less plastic, create a positive scroll, have intentional info coming in, or have less on the schedule. Try something new in your environment and see what it feels like or changes in your life.

What emotions does your environment evoke?

What might add more life or 'you' to your environment?

Perfection is not the goal. As humans, we are ever-growing and have strengths and weaknesses. The normality of life is having ups and downs. We can be a part of life, live each day the best way we know how, and continue to figure things out one step at a time. We have empowering options in these nine areas of our lives. We need to take a look at them with awareness, edit our patterns, cultivate new habits that we desire one step at a time, and add tools to our toolbox for when the next speed bump, volcano, or celebration shows up on our doorstep. Our bodies, minds, and spirits will be able to handle it, be present in it, and even live with a bit more liberated ease.

Whether you are noticing whispers, yells, or two-by-fours in your body, mind, soul, or life, you deserve to commit to change. It can start with one microhabitat at a time, and the drastic change over time could result in the best version of you. Addressing any of these critical areas and making conscious choices can enhance your physical, mental, and emotional health, leading to a more fulfilling and balanced life.

What's one small thing you can do this week to start feeling your best?

About the Author

Emily Marquis is an NBC-HWC Clinical Health Coach with an MA in Health & Wellness Coaching with a background in human resources. She is a professor and mentor in integrated health sciences in several NBHWC programs including mindbodygreen, Emory University, Northwestern Health Sciences University, UC San Diego, and University of Vermont.

Emily has been a health coach on research teams with the University of Louisville and Dartmouth College. She is also a certified Yoga & Mindfulness Consultant. Her mission is to support patient, clients, organizations, and students in feeling their best by cultivating health habits their way in various settings. In her private practice, she focuses on mentoring coaches and serving clients by partnering with therapists and clinics to support mental health. She lives in southwest Colorado with her family, loving the balance of an outdoor adventure and listening to good podcast inside.

Connect with Emily

LinkedIn: www.LinkedIn.com/in/EmilyMarquisco/

Website: www.EmilyMarquis.com

Email: emily@emilymarquis.com

Instagram: @emily_marquis_celebrates

Facebook: www.Facebook.com/officialemilymarquis

Free Consultation:
https://calendly.com/emilymarquis/freeconsultation

A Resilient Warrior: My Journey Through Life's Trials

By Peggy Beneby

"Get a chair for mom," a nurse yelled down the hall. The hospital ER hallway was cold and dim. I stood there, numb, outside the room where my daughter lay after her car accident. She had broken bones in both legs and her pelvis, a ruptured spleen, and something called "road rash" from being thrown from the car. Glass and asphalt were tangled in her hair, and bruises covered her body. Seeing her lying there on the gurney made my knees weak. A nurse brought me a chair and a blanket. I could hear machines beeping and doctors' voices. They needed my consent for surgeries and bombarded me with questions: Who else was in the car? What was my relationship to them?

It was July 3, 2012, my birthday. I had just wrapped up a business meeting where I was the closing speaker and had been invited out for a birthday drink with my colleague. It was close to midnight, and I was thinking I should be heading home. That's when I got the call from my daughter's father. "There's been an accident. Don't panic. We don't know what happened, but meet me at Albany Medical Hospital." My heart dropped. I rushed to the hospital, trying to stay optimistic. It's just a fender bender, I kept telling myself. They went to the hospital to check for injuries, I hoped. But deep down, I feared something much worse.

The week before, my daughter had gone to spend time with her older sister Ro, her father's child from before we met. Ro had a son born one month before my daughter. Because it was my birthday, my daughter wanted to return to Albany to be with me. I knew they would all be driving back together, but I couldn't have imagined what had happened.

I was sitting in that cold, dim hallway when I saw her father. I asked, "How is Ro?" The hospital staff wouldn't give me any information about anyone but my daughter. I didn't know the other people in the car besides Ro and her son. Her father looked me in the face and said, "She's dead." It didn't register. "Don't play with me," I replied, desperate for it to be a sick joke. "I'm not playing. She's dead." The world spun. I needed another chair.

This happened on the heels of my battle with breast cancer in 2011. I thought that was a tough fight. After battling my daughter's father for divorce, custody, and child support, I had to fight breast cancer. I had just finished several surgeries, chemo, radiation, blood transfusions, and 12 months of hormone-blocking infusions. My life had been turned upside down, and all normalcy was interrupted for an entire year. Now it was turning again.

She was in the ICU for weeks, and they took such good care of her. I never left her side for more than a few hours. If I wasn't there, a member of my ministry team was. Once she was moved to the general hospital children's ward, I thought the road would get easier, but it got much harder. Even though my daughter was a mature, independent 12-year-old, she needed more of my care and attention.

For at least a month, all I did was wake up and go to the hospital. Friends came to see me there. My daughter had friends and family visit her daily. I felt so blessed, considering the circumstances. I was already on disability due to my cancer diagnosis. I had completed my licenses and certifications to offer financial services. I had flexibility of time and the support of many. It was over 30 days that my daughter spent in the hospital. After several surgeries and procedures, we found out she would be non-weight-bearing for another six weeks. The hospital recommended inpatient rehab in a facility that specialized in children, but it was a 30-minute drive from where we lived. It would be difficult for family and friends to visit. She didn't want to go. She wasn't there long due to pain management issues and abdominal pain. She was readmitted to the hospital. This time, they wanted to send her home. Home?! But she still needed so much care! We had to install a ramp to our apartment. She needed a hospital bed, wheelchair, commode, injections—argh! "I'm not a nurse," I rebutted. How could I be expected to care for her? "I don't like needles, and you want me to give her shots?" No way! They can't be serious, I thought. Well, they were serious, and home we went once I had everything in place. It reminded me of when I was expecting. I wasn't ready then, either. The thought of being a parent was daunting enough without the thought of giving birth. I read the book "What to Expect When You're Expecting," but I still didn't know what to expect. I couldn't imagine how much joy and fulfillment I would feel after giving birth. Yet I was still nervous to take her home then. Well, I resolved that if I was strong enough to care for her as an infant, I could do this too.

As a kid, I used to like this ride at Rye Playland called the "ROTOR." It was a ride that spun so fast you stuck to the wall, and then the floor would drop from under your feet. After a couple of minutes, the floor would rise, and the spinning would slow down, releasing us from the wall. I found it thrilling then, but this time I did not know how low the floor was or when my life would stop spinning. Yet, there was something familiar about it. I had felt that way before. It was like when I realized the man I fell in love with and married would break my heart. My daughter's father and I were not going to work out despite my wanting so badly for us to be the happy family I longed for. Unfortunately, we did not have a happy marriage. In fact, it went south rather quickly. After a failed marriage and a difficult divorce, I spent my days focused on being the best mom I could be to my child. I spent all my time and money on her. Whatever I needed to do to provide, she was not lacking for anything.

I had to be strong for my daughter. It's always been for her! I guess I was always a warrior at heart. I had worked full-time and gone to school full-time for my bachelor's degree. The only difference with my Master's was that I was a single parent. I began to rebuild my self-esteem and financial life. Despite lacking financial education and making poor decisions financially, I was determined. It wasn't long before I was in a debt cycle and living paycheck to paycheck, "robbing Peter to pay Paul," as they say. I thought going back to school would help, so I could get paid a higher salary and have better opportunities. I was taking classes for a second Master's and thinking about applying for my doctorate when I was introduced to the financial services industry. I am thankful that I became self-employed. I had a flexible schedule and learned concepts of how money works that allowed me to get back on my feet after life's challenges.

After my daughter was walking again and going to outpatient rehab, I met with the orthopedist to see how she was progressing. He stated, "The good news is, she is young, and her body is resilient." Ah, that word "resilient" rang out in my mind. It meant that, in time, her body would heal despite the trauma. "While there will be scars, she will essentially be able to do everything she could have done before the accident," the doctor continued. The biggest challenge then was getting her to believe that her legs were totally healed and she could put full weight on them. While she could run and jump, my daughter continued to suffer from pain management and anxiety years after this event. Her body was healed, but how resilient was her mind?

During this time, my daughter also fell into a deep depression. She did not want to go out or spend time with friends. When she finally went back to school, she was not her inquisitive, happy self. She lacked the desire and attention for her studies she once had. She was also not agreeable to counseling. It's amazing that while her body was completely healed, we still had to work on her mind, her attitude, and her beliefs. It's like an internal war that battles what you know and what you feel. Thankfully, she had a strong foundation. The same foundation I had. God's love. That's why I named her Theodora, meaning "Gift of God."

Why do I consider myself a resilient warrior, you might ask? A resilient warrior is someone who gets up every day and faces challenges regardless of emotions. A resilient warrior understands that each day is a new day and an opportunity to live your best life. Even when I did not always feel like a resilient warrior, my instinct for it was always there. In fact, when my daughter was finally back on her feet and back to school, I was a puddle. Physically and mentally drained and in pain. I felt like I needed my own hospital bed the entire time I was nursing my daughter back to full recovery. I must have kept up a strong facade, but inside I was scared, tired, and not feeling very resilient. I felt like I didn't have much time to process my recovery journey from breast cancer, and now I was forced to process my daughter's pain. Hadn't she been through enough, thinking she could lose me to cancer? How does one process losing her sister and knowing she could have also died in the same accident? She was angry and bitter, with a lot of anxiety. I did not know how to help her because I needed help myself. I sought counseling for both of us. I had my friends, family, and faith leaders to lean on, but I had to find my own resilience and fight through it. Throughout my life, I learned to lean on my faith. Today, I wake up with daily devotions, write in my journal, and read motivational books. I have incredible mentors and coaches in business and ministry. I read books and listen to audios by motivational speakers like Les Brown and John Maxwell. Each day is a new opportunity for growth.

What are some things that are resilient?

My daughter, like all children, was resilient. There's something amazing about the capacity of children to heal. I admire that in them. Like their small bodies are still developing and adjusting to the world, their minds and spirits have a unique ability to bend and not break. This natural resilience is a gift, and I've seen it in my daughter as she fought through her pain and trauma. Today, you would never know all that she had been through and we are so close because of it.

What does resilience mean?

Resilience is the ability to withstand adversity and bounce back from difficult life events. It's not just about surviving but also about thriving despite challenges. In my life, resilience has been about facing the unexpected with courage, adapting to new realities, and moving forward even when the path is unclear or the floor drops from beneath my feet.

What does it mean to be a warrior?

Being a warrior means having the strength and courage to fight through life's battles. It means standing up to life's challenges and not backing down, even when the odds seem insurmountable. Warriors have a determination that keeps them going, a fire inside that doesn't easily extinguish. In my journey, I've had to be a warrior for my daughter, for myself, and for the future I want to build. It means making tough decisions, staying focused on what's important, and always pushing forward, no matter how hard things get.

In conclusion, my journey has been marked by trials that tested my strength and resolve. From fighting breast cancer to caring for my daughter after her devastating accident, each challenge has shaped me into a resilient warrior. I've learned that resilience is not just about bouncing back but also about growing stronger with each experience. It's about finding the inner strength to keep moving forward, even when the road is tough. Through it all, my faith, family, and friends have been my pillars of support. I've discovered that being a warrior means having the courage to face adversity head-on, the resilience to keep going, and the wisdom to learn and grow from every challenge.

About the Author

Peggy Beneby, M.S.Ed. is an educator and financial professional based in Westchester County, NY.

Her career began in secondary education and youth development, where she worked as a teacher, tutor, and youth pastor. She later transitioned to higher education administration at the University at Albany, focusing on residential life and staff development. Today, Peggy, along with her daughter, is passionate about teaching financial literacy to help close the wealth gap. She runs her own financial services team, trains future leaders, and is a licensed New York State Life Insurance Instructor and Licensing Coach.

Connect With Peggy

https://calendly.com/teambenebypfs/meeting-with-peggy-beneby

LinkedIn.com/in/Peggy-Beneby-b41b9270

https://livemore.net/mbeneby

Instagram @smart.moneymovess

TheRealHowMoneyWorks.com/us/beneby

Bulletproof:
How to Build a Mindset
to Overcome Any Challenge

By Glen Henderson

"The greatest discovery of my generation is that a human being can alter his life by altering his attitudes of mind."

~ William James

"So, the test results are in: you have cancer."

Did you feel that?

That knot in your gut when you read those words?

You may not have had cancer yourself, or known anyone close to you who has, but I'll guarantee you know someone who is, right now, facing a major challenge. It might be a major project they've been assigned at their job—an assignment they may not have the confidence to complete successfully. They may have just lost their job and are unsure about their future prospects. They may be struggling with a breakup or a divorce, especially if they feel that it was their own fault. They might be faced with a health issue of some kind and feeling fear beginning to take hold. Who knows, the "they" might be YOU.

You're thinking about it right now, aren't you? So how are you going to deal with it? Stand up to it? Overcome it? The first battle you'll need to win is very close to home. In fact, it's right between your ears. I know because that's where MY battle was. You see, I was the one who heard that news.

My wife and I heard the diagnosis together, sitting in the office of my haggard-looking oncologist (more on that later), and at that moment, I had a decision to make. Do I sink into fear and despair? Do I "get my affairs in order?" Do I withdraw from life and retreat into focusing on my own struggles?

Do I give up?

The answer to all these questions was given to me more than 50 years before that diagnosis. For my 10th birthday, my parents gave me two very important gifts:

- A beautiful leather-bound Bible (with my name embossed in gold—fancy!)

- A book by Charles T. Jones called "Life Is Tremendous."

Having grown up in a Christian home and family, the value of the Bible was self-explanatory. Reading "Life Is Tremendous" changed everything for me. It taught me that it's possible to live life with a positive, optimistic attitude ... ALL THE TIME.

Does that sound weird to you? Pollyanna-ish? "Unrealistic?" I understand. Most people feel the same way but catch this—it's important:

YOUR ATTITUDE IS UP TO YOU.

It's YOUR choice. YOU get to decide how you will think, how you will view life, and how you will react to every circumstance. And you're about to learn three steps to build the kind of mindset that will empower you to overcome nearly any challenge.

STEP ONE: MAKE A DECISION

When the doctor said those words to me, I had two immediate reactions. My first thought was:

"Wow—this is going to make a great topic for my next book!" (True story. And it really will—that book is coming soon.)

My next thought was almost at the same time as the first but MUCH more powerful:

Alright then, the game begins.

And the game is ALREADY WON.

With my faith, my phenomenal support system of friends and family, and my superior state of mind, this battle is already over.

It's done—finished!

Cancer is gonna get GOT!

Now then, whom do I need to gather for my medical team to make it happen?

Does that sound too arrogant to you? Too cocky? If it does, consider this: As I mentioned before, it's possible to choose your state of mind at any time. You can choose negativity and defeat, or you can choose to look at the best possible outcome. If it's not a way of thinking you're used to, it may take some practice, but you can start from where you are. After all, it IS your choice—why not choose the positive?

"But Glen, that's not realistic!" Trust me, I KNEW I had cancer. Realistic enough for you? Here's the difference: I never allowed that diagnosis to define me. I'M the one who gets to define me. Never— NEVER—allow fear or doubt to enter your thoughts. Tough task? Let me share a way to do it.

STEP TWO: CHOOSE YOUR TEAM CAREFULLY

Remember my second response to the cancer news?

"Whom do I need to gather for my medical team to make it happen?"

If you're facing a major challenge, especially one that's going to require you to maintain a superior attitude, the last thing you need is to have anyone—ANYONE—around you who doesn't share your mental commitment.

We consulted with a number of medical professionals in the city where we live—and in many cases we found a frustrating lack of optimism. In one case, the doctor we met with walked into the room with unkempt hair, deep bags under his eyes, and wearing a wrinkled lab coat, looking for all the world like a college freshman who'd just pulled an all-nighter before final exams. Every time we asked him a question, we were greeted with long pauses and heavy sighs—as if either he didn't know the answer or he was afraid to say something wrong. Needless to say, he was NOT asked to be part of my medical team. In fact, I chose to go across the country until I found an institution and a group of medical professionals who were "down" with my mindset—because anyone who wasn't didn't get to be on my medical team.

That mental connection was a major factor in the completion of my cancer project because it meant that I didn't have to fight against my caregivers' attitudes to maintain my own.

STEP THREE: DO THE WORK

You do know that just sitting around "thinking positive" isn't going to accomplish anything. Whatever your project or challenge you need to overcome is, you're going to need to work. Hard.

You probably don't need me to tell you the tasks you'll need to complete along the way, just don't fool yourself into thinking that you're not going to have to give them everything you've got.

I busted my chops to complete the various facets of my cancer treatment. We packed up and moved across the country to live near the cancer treatment facility in Phoenix, Arizona, for six solid weeks. I tolerated radiation treatments five days a week. I worked out SEVEN days a week. I changed my diet. I made myself go to bed earlier and get more sleep (and as one of the original New York night owls, you can imagine how much I loved THAT). I spent the following 22 (and counting) months flying back and forth between Houston and Phoenix for follow-up visits. I endured over two years of medications that made it nearly impossible to lose weight, even with the daily workouts. I put two major business ventures on hold in order to prioritize my recovery and health above all else. Was the work worth it? You tell me. At my follow-up visit in May of 2024, I received the word: CURED.

Cancer-free.

Look, obviously, everyone's experience with cancer is different. Far be it from me to guarantee anyone that "all you've gotta do is think right and you TOO..."

Heck no.

But here's the question that I think is important: Would I have been able to overcome my cancer and find a cure if I HADN'T first conquered my mindset? I don't know, and to tell you the truth, I don't need to know.

You know why? Because I DID it.

Know what else? So can you.

Here's a good place to start: Begin to get control of what you allow into your mind by reading the right kinds of books. A few I recommend are:

- *Life is Tremendous* (my first), by Charles T. Jones
- The 15 Invaluable Laws of Growth, by John C. Maxwell
- Empower Your Thoughts, by Scott Allan.

Start your journey toward a positive attitude today and start reaping results tomorrow.

"Having a positive attitude isn't wishy-washy, it's a concrete and intelligent way to view problems, challenges, and obstacles."

~ Jeff Moore

About the Author

Glen Henderson is a singer, author, speaker, investor, and personal development coach.

He can tell you exactly where he was on September 8, 1966, when *Star Trek* first appeared on TV screens across America.

His first two books, *All I Need To Know About Success I Learned From Star Trek* and *It's Not About The Destination: Life Lessons From Star Trek,* share the treasures of wisdom and life lessons to be found within the *Trek* universe ... if you know where to look.

He's currently developing an executive coaching program teaching entrepreneurs, corporate leaders, and motivated professionals how to maximize their leadership potential by learning from the inspiration of the great Captains of *Star Trek.*

He lives in Houston, Texas with his wife Paula Wigley and their tuxedo cats Sam and Rosic.

Connect with Glen

Email: glen@thetrekwhisperer.com

Seven Principles of Excellence

By Floyd McLendon Jr.

Character, integrity, mental resilience, and a commitment to personal growth have forged my journey to becoming a man of substance and a significant contributor to society. For the past 34 years, this path has been anything but conventional. I faced setbacks, such as flunking out of college and pursuing a professional basketball career before becoming a U.S. Navy SEAL. I served 25 years in the United States Navy, overcame severe physical trauma, and emerged as an inspirational keynote speaker. Today, I am also an ambassador for a traumatic brain injury treatment program for military veterans and first responders, serve as the Director of Institutional Advancement at a leading chiropractic university, and fulfill my role as a city councilman.

The blueprint behind my success is a frequent topic of discussion. My response has consistently highlighted seven principles shaping my approach to expected and unforeseen life challenges: Commitment, Sacrifice, House in Order, Master the Basics, Consistency, Attention to Detail, and Exclusivity. These principles form the bedrock of my journey, enabling me to navigate obstacles and achieve my objectives across personal and professional realms.

Commitment: The Foundation of Success

Embarking on my journey to become a Navy SEAL, I had yet to learn what the profession entailed, except that it was mentally and physically demanding. At that point in my life, I was searching for a purpose and found it quickly. The first step towards excellence was making a conscious decision to commit fully. This commitment transcends a simple declaration; it is a profound belief in one's capabilities and the process ahead. It involves trusting your coaches, teammates, and the system designed to guide you.

When you commit, you promise yourself and those around you that you will give your best effort. This dedication requires unwavering faith in your ability to succeed and in the methodologies that will help you achieve your goals, regardless of others' belief in you, even from your inner circle. It is about owning your path and taking full responsibility for your progress, knowing that every step is part of a larger plan toward achieving greatness.

This principle applies equally to the corporate world and sports arena. In both settings, genuine commitment means dedicating yourself wholeheartedly to your goals and embracing the journey with confidence and determination. Committing fully sets the stage for extraordinary achievements and inspires those around you to do the same.

Sacrifice: The Price of Excellence

Understanding and embracing the sacrifices necessary for success is crucial. These sacrifices must be crystal clear, whether mental, verbal, or visual. Mentally, it may mean pushing through fatigue and staying focused when distractions arise. Verbally, it involves positive self-talk and avoiding negative influences. Visually, it could mean envisioning your goals and the steps needed to achieve them. Accepting these sacrifices requires a mindset at peace with giving up certain comforts or conveniences. It means recognizing that the path to excellence often involves difficult choices and being willing to make those choices consistently.

From age 11, my dream was to become a professional basketball player. By 26, I was well on my way, having played All-Navy Basketball and receiving an invitation to play All-Armed Forces. My ultimate sacrifice was redirecting all my time, energy, and focus toward becoming a U.S. Navy SEAL. This decision meant sacrificing a goal I had pursued for 15 years, yet my heart was at peace with it. True sacrifice is about prioritizing long-term goals over short-term pleasures and understanding that these sacrifices are integral to the journey.

In the professional and sports arenas, true success requires an unwavering commitment to sacrifices. It's about making difficult choices that align with your long-term vision and being at peace with the paths you choose. This mindset separates the good from the great, and it's a testament to the strength and resilience needed to achieve excellence.

House in Order: Life and Career

To fully devote 100% of your mental and physical energy to your craft, it is essential to ensure everything outside your profession is in order. House in Order includes maintaining healthy relationships with your spouse, children, family, and friends. Stable personal relationships provide a robust support system that enhances your professional focus. Financial stability is also critical; worrying about money can be a significant distraction. You can concentrate on your professional responsibilities without additional stress by ensuring your finances are well-managed.

Additionally, clearly defining and fulfilling your role responsibilities at home—whether it's taking care of vehicles, being a supportive spouse, or being an attentive parent—helps create a balanced life. In my household, I've created a binder detailing all of my responsibilities. It's written in such detail that my 16-year-old son would be able to execute them in the unlikely event something were to happen to me. This balance is key to giving your all to your professional endeavors, empowering you to feel in control and confident without feeling overwhelmed by external pressures.

Creating this balance is crucial in the professional and sports arenas. When your personal life is in order, you can channel all your energy into your craft, knowing that your foundational support systems are solid. This preparation and foresight bolster your professional performance and ensure you are fully present.

Master the Basics: Building a Strong Foundation

Mastering the basics is essential to achieving excellence in any field. *To truly excel, your mental and physical capabilities within your profession should far surpass what is required during actual performance.* This demands rigorous training and a relentless commitment to improving your foundational skills. It's about reaching a certain level and continuously striving for improvement. This could mean perfecting fundamental techniques until they become second nature in sports. In the business world, it might involve mastering the core principles of your industry.

I experienced this firsthand when I decided to become a U.S. Navy SEAL. Despite not knowing how to swim, I trained intensively and, after six months, barely passed the Basic Underwater Demolition/ SEAL screening test. Three and a half years later, I advanced to becoming a Search and Rescue Swimmer, and two years after that, I earned my place as a U.S. Navy SEAL. This journey underscores that a solid foundation enables you to tackle more complex challenges confidently.

The basics are the bedrock of what are often considered advanced skills. With a thorough understanding and proficiency in these foundational areas, reaching higher performance levels is attainable. Consistently revisiting and refining these basic skills ensures they remain sharp and reliable, providing the strength to excel in more complex and demanding scenarios.

Consistency: The Key to Long-Term Success

Consistency is the cornerstone of long-term success. To truly achieve excellence, you must commit to consistent, focused daily practice sustained over an extended period. This means relentlessly addressing your weaknesses while continually enhancing your strengths.

In 2008, during my selection process for a Tier One Special Warfare Team, I experienced firsthand the power of consistency. Our training consisted of relentless shooting and moving drills for the first eight weeks. We practiced shooting in the morning, took breaks for lunch and dinner, and continued well into the night. This intense regimen ingrained in me the profound importance of consistent effort.

Such dedication sharpens your skills and builds essential qualities like discipline and resilience. The daily commitment to repetitive actions and continuous improvement ultimately leads to mastery. This principle applies not just to physical training but also to mental preparation. Developing routines that keep you focused, motivated, and ready to perform at your best ensures that these consistent efforts yield significant improvements and sustained excellence over time.

Attention to Detail: The Art of Precision

Mastering the small nuances and being meticulous in your actions and communication can distinguish the exceptional from the average. Attention to detail means breaking down tasks into smaller, manageable steps and executing each with precision.

During my time with the SEAL Teams, I took the standard of organization to the highest level. My locker was so meticulously arranged that any teammate could locate any clothing or gear simply by referring to my 'locker binder,' which cataloged everything. This level of organization not only ensures that nothing is overlooked but also fosters a sense of pride, knowing that every aspect of your performance is fine-tuned.

Whether you're perfecting a sports technique or managing a complex project at work, attention to detail is crucial. It involves clear, effective communication to ensure that everyone involved understands your intentions and expectations. By focusing on these finer points, you can identify areas for improvement, make necessary adjustments, and elevate your performance to new heights.

Exclusivity: Fostering Cohesion—Individual/Team

Consciously limiting external distractions—such as people, places, social media, and activities—is crucial for cultivating team cohesion and maintaining focus. Individuals and teams can concentrate on their shared goals and work together more effectively by minimizing these distractions.

From my personal experience, I've found that intentional exclusivity, such as going off the grid when deeply focused on a goal, can foster stronger team connections. This deliberate act of focusing on shared objectives leads to more time spent together and collective problem-solving. Overcoming challenges as a team further solidifies these relationships, creating a strong foundation of unity and mutual support.

When team members limit exposure to external influences, they can fully commit to their collaborative efforts and shared objectives. This focused environment nurtures collaboration, builds trust, and strengthens camaraderie, each of which are essential for achieving team success and exccllence.

Conclusion

Embracing the seven core principles—Commitment, Sacrifice, House in Order, Mastering the Basics, Consistency, Attention to Detail, and Exclusivity—creates a robust foundation for achieving excellence. Each principle is interlinked, reinforcing and amplifying the others to foster a comprehensive approach to success. By integrating these values, you can elevate your performance and enhance the collective strength of any team or organization. Commitment to these principles and dedication to ongoing improvement pave the way for reaching your highest potential and driving unparalleled success.

I apply these principles daily, confident that they will continue to elevate all facets of my life, allowing me to leverage my God-given talents fully. This commitment fuels my ongoing journey of service to you, our community, and the world, driving me to achieve excellence in every endeavor.

About the Author

Floyd McLendon Jr. is the Director of Institutional Advancement at Parker University. Additionally, Floyd is the Ambassador for The INVICTA Project at Parker Performance Institute. This groundbreaking program offers comprehensive treatments in neurological, physiological, and integrative healthcare, specifically tailored for military veterans and first responders affected by traumatic brain injuries.

Floyd honorably served in the United States Navy for over 25 years, including 15 years as a U.S. Navy SEAL. He embarked on five deployments spanning five continents, playing a pivotal role in establishing strategic presences in 24 countries. Floyd's leadership within the SEAL Teams earned him recognition as a prominent national speaker for the Naval Special Warfare Community. His presentations delved into the leadership and mental toughness strategies vital for achieving mission success, showcasing his expertise and dedication to service.

Floyd proudly calls the Great State of Texas his home. Actively engaged in federal and state political spheres, he passionately advocates for initiatives supporting military veterans and first responders. His commitment to civic duty further demonstrates his service as a city councilman in McLendon-Chisholm, TX.

Floyd is esteemed as a professional speaker and published author. He is known for his expertise in developing, implementing, and evaluating programs that drive positive change for corporations and individuals seeking professional and personal growth. His unwavering dedication to serving humanity is evident in these roles, earning him widespread respect and admiration.

Connect with Floyd

LinkedIn: www.LinkedIn.com/in/legendtree/

How to Speak Anywhere, Anytime, to Anyone

By Judith Field

Speaking in front of crowds is supposed to be scarier than anything else—even death. I, too, was a shy child, but I remember how, when I was ten, I found my voice.

It was out playing cricket in the backyard with my brothers. As the only girl and the youngest of three children, I seemed to be always fielding and was quickly bowled out by the big boys.

I put up with that for months. However, one day, I suddenly approached Lloyd, my older brother and, putting my hands on my hips, I looked up at him and said, "Lloyd, I want to bat twice and I want you and Ian to bowl underarm. Not grubbers!"

Well. He looked at me daggers, and I thought he was going to smack me. But he just threw his head back and laughed and called out to Ian, "The little brat is right. How soft do we bowl?"

That day I changed from a shy little girl into an assertive person who stood her ground and spoke up. And I have not stopped. What's that got to do with public speaking, I hear you ask?

Everything.

You see, getting up and speaking has more to do with how you speak than what you say. It's more about confidence than talent, though knowing what to do and how to do it is vital. Let's get started to help you be confident, clear, and concise when you need to speak.

If you are willing to put the following tips into your speaking, you will reap the benefits. I know from personal experience. In 2015 I joined Rostrum, an international public speaking group. I had already been teaching public speaking to students and staff in over 200 schools and trained corporates and business people all over Victoria and was even invited to teach university students in Hong Kong. So, I put up my hand to go into the state's public speaking competition. It was a 10-minute speech and I received a huge amount of support and encouragement from my club. I was the last speaker of the night and pretty nervous. However, I got up and stood in front of 100 people and three judges and put into practice what Rostrum coaches had suggested.

I won!

The confidence and skills I gained that night helped my career, confidence and capacity to speak anywhere, any time to anyone. So read on!

So, what is public speaking?

Most people think it's about the words. However, by themselves, the words only contribute 10% to your meaning. The main part of speaking, believe it or not, is our body language. What you do with your posture, eye contact, facial expressions, gestures, feet, and hands conveys over 60% of your message. Hence, your body must look relaxed and natural.

My first tip therefore is: FAKE IT TILL YOU MAKE IT!

The other thing is not to fiddle, move too much, or look nervous. The body will convey about 60% no matter what. So, make it work for you.

The art of eye contact is tricky. Looking at the audience while you speak is vital. However, for some people, that is very difficult. Think about them not looking at you or you not looking at them. What will happen? If you do not look at them, you cannot engage with them. If you want to engage with your audience, the main way is through connecting with their eyes. They are the window to the soul and far less scary if you see the audience as friends, not foes.

The second most important part of speaking is your voice variety. There are many aspects of voice. Five important ones begin with the letter P. Pitch, pace, pauses, pronunciation, and projection. Then, there is emphasis, diction, timbre, and volume. The way you say a sentence can change its whole meaning. Try saying, "I didn't say she said it," seven different ways...

The voice contributes about 30% of your message, and hence, the more you change it, the more interesting your speech will be. If you have ever heard a boring speaker, chances are they are too monotonous in their voice variety. I suggest you watch a couple of TED talks. All of their speakers speak brilliantly, and their voice variety will be excellent; all of them.

A tip about pace and pauses: There is actually an ideal speed to speak at to be the most effective. It's 120 words per minute. That tip alone is an important one, because now you know how many words to write for the length of the talk! As for pauses, these are IMPORTANT. You must pause often. Here are the main places to pause: after a rhetorical question, after each point, for dramatic effect, when you need to look at your notes, and when you need to take a breath. Most nervous speakers rush their speeches... don't!

What about the words? These need to be short, sharp, and simple. Generally speaking, the shorter the word, the easier it is to say. The other thing about words is that the most important word in a speech is "you." This means you are likely to connect with your audience.

Figurative language enhances speaking (and writing). Metaphors are magical. They create pictures in the listener's mind. They are concise and can be clever if not cliche. Similes are similar. They need to be original. As cold as ice is boring, as cold as snow is more original. Alliteration ads spice. I once said, "I sat on the train and let racism run rampant." Alliteration is memorable. That's why "Use water wisely" is much better than "Use water carefully."

My favourite is onomatopoeia. "Bang!" or "Snap" or a click of the fingers can be more effective and shorter than saying, "There was a sudden change."

The main thing with words is that you need a mix of logical ones and emotional ones. For example, sentences such as, "It makes sense that... "should be followed soon after by ones like, "It makes me sad that..." That way, you appeal to the heads and hearts of your audience.

Now, let's look at structure. Structure is vital in speaking. The words go out and disappear like a magic rug. Hence, you must signal and signpost so your audience can follow your train of thought. The basic structure is:

1. Grab 'em.

2. Tell 'em what you want to tell 'em.

3. Tell 'em what you told 'em.

Finish with a bang.

This advice is not original, but very solid.

There are many structures. Three simple ones are:

1. Past, present, and future.

Spokes wheel: A central idea, followed by a point and illustration, back to the central idea, out to another idea, and then back to the main theme again, etc.

A change of focus from personal to broader and then an international focus.

It's important to grab your audience's attention from the start. So, what makes a sizzling start? Some ideas that you might try include using a rhetorical question or two, a quote, an image, an anecdote, or a statistic.

Although the beginning and, of course, the middle are important, the end is the most important. You must finish with a flourish, not a whimper. Do not finish with "Thank you." It's polite but weak. Finish with a quote, a call for action, or alliteration. Any of these will be much more memorable.

Practice is vital. The more you practice, the better. Most people only practice three times. No, that is not enough. Try practising 13 times, as if. As if means that you need to see yourself in front of the real audience every time you practice.

Practice also helps to reduce your nerves. Being nervous is natural. You are the centre of attention when you speak. Learn to accept that, whether you are an introvert or an extrovert. I wrote at the start to "Fake it till you make it." Indeed, if you know what you are talking about and have practised 13 times as if, you are less likely to be as nervous as you would normally be. Finally, tell the negative voice in your head to go away, as it will muck you up if you let it.

Although you need to be well rehearsed, try not to learn it off by heart. It could sound singsong and not natural. Also, have notes or cards handy so you can look at them and not freeze if you do forget anything.

Finally, be aware of your purpose and audience. They shape what you say and how you say it. A persuasive speech aims to change their view on a topic. An instructional speech needs to tell them how to do, make, or be something. An informative speech, as it says, hopes to educate people. A comedic speech tries to entertain them. As for audiences, they are not all the same. They can be specialists, meaning you can use jargon. If they are children, do not use big words. And remember, if it's a general audience, appeal to universal human emotions.

Public speaking is one of the most essential skills in life. We need it every day. The way we communicate with our family, friends, and colleagues can make all the difference. In today's world of devices, AI, and heads on screens, it's even more important to be able to speak up and be heard.

I wrote at the start about how I overcame my shyness and learned to be assertive. What I need to tell you now is why this skill is so important to me and should be to you.

I became a secondary English teacher in 1969! I fell into teaching almost accidentally. Yet, within a day or two, I became passionate about teaching teenagers to be confident, competent communicators. I made some public speaking errors in the early days.

I used to try to get control by shouting louder than the class. That not only made my voice hoarse, but it also made the class more excited and rowdy. My mentor came in and whispered, "A calm teacher and a quiet one helps the class be calm and quiet."

I never forgot that advice.

I'm still teaching English privately as well as running my public speaking business, and I'm still just as passionate. It's a skill that is needed more and more, particularly post-COVID.

So many people seem to have lost their confidence and direction. Many teens and adults feel uncertain about their future (and the future of the world). We need to believe in ourselves and our ability to navigate through life even more now than when I was a teen. The ability to speak anywhere, to anyone, and anytime has never been more important.

Now, I have a message for any teens who might decide to read this book (unlikely, but I'm an optimist). Here goes. GET OFF THOSE SCREENS!

I SAID: Get off those screens!

They are stopping you from real communication! And they are mashing your brain! Democracy depends on citizens who can sort fact from fiction and who can listen, speak, and communicate. Harangue over, but truly we all need to communicate effectively.

These tips work. I have helped thousands of people, from primary and secondary students to CEOs and whole companies. The art of speaking is going to become even more essential as we move into the robot age. So, to get the edge and reach your full potential, use words wisely, confidently, and deliberately. Or as I finish my workshops and coaching sessions: Say what you mean, mean what you say, and never be mean when you say it.

About the Author

Judith Field is an outstanding, experienced trainer and presenter in the area of presentation skills and English. Coming from an educational background, she combines skill, humour, stories, practical tips and interaction to shift her participants from where they are to where they can be in the area of speaking. Judith has already published a public speaking book called _Speech Matters._ Judith's clients include: 190 schools, 30 large businesses and many non for profits.

Judith has also taught English for over 40 years and her students often keep in touch with her for years.

She helped found a primary school and was Head of English at a leading secondary school. Her passion for education is boundless. Her tutoring business is full, based on satisfied customers' recommendations.

In 2015, Judith joined Rostrum, a public speaking group for business people. She volunteered to go in the state competition. And won it. Since then, Judith has become a coach in Rostrum and is often called upon to give feedback. Her comments are received well as she manages to pinpoint what speakers do well and why and where and how they can improve.

Judith practises what she preaches!

Connect with Judith

Website: www.directspeech.com.au

Embracing Vulnerability: The Courage to be Authentic and Share Your Story

By Shakira Taylor

Before delving into the rewards of embracing vulnerability, I must share some of my personal journey in finding the courage to be authentic when everything in the world tells you to be anything but yourself. By giving you this part of myself, I hope I will immediately remove the barrier between us, open your heart to hear, and encourage your spirit to keep reading. This is my intention.

For the first 25 years of my life, who I thought I was supposed to be kept me going. The need to survive set the speed limit, and controlling my environment was the driver of my life. As a young adult, the pressure to survive, come out unharmed, and remain accomplished yet disconnected from myself and others in an unsafe world was the mission. I was not aware of why my disconnection from the world was filled with such uncertainties, but deep in my heart lived a sense of peace and a profound connection to a higher power. For many of those 25 years, I recall repeating the same prayer: "Lord, show me how to exist in both the physical and the spiritual dimensions!" Today, I still have the same prayer, just from a different heart space.

Why did the world feel unsafe and disconnected? Where was this belief coming from? Did something happen in my early years that led me to assign a negative meaning to the world? Reflecting on this, it took me a while to become aware that the world kept proving my beliefs about my disconnection. If the law of vibration, which states that everything corresponds to a specific rate of frequency held in mind, was true, then I was the poster person, as life kept proving itself to me. The thoughts that dominated my mind were "I don't belong," "I am not worthy," and "I'm not smart or good enough." These beliefs left me paralyzed with fear, blocking me from sharing my voice, raising my hand, trying new things, and connecting with others.

Questions about my personal feelings, the world, and even other people's resilience to live fully each day flooded my mind. What did people value? What were my own values? How were they navigating life and still exuding what I perceived as joy, community, and abundance? What would it take for me to live courageously, powerfully, and freely? I yearned for answers as I started on the path of self-discovery and self-love, beginning with the Asking Journey Method. The asking journey method calls for one to elevate the power of the questions they ask themselves, others, and a higher power. The practice allows you to ask for help and support when needed. It encourages you to identify the areas in your life where your needs are not being met and to set up structures to meet those needs. The asking journey method is necessary self-work that forces people to get clear and honest with themselves.

My mother encouraged me to explore my thoughts about life. She listened to my questions even when the answers were not readily available. She stimulated my interest by surrounding me with books to read and gave me the most life-changing mantra to affirm daily:

"You were not created with a spirit of fear, but of power, love and a sound mind" (English Standard Version Bible, 2001, 2 Tim 1:7).

In the process of reading and listening to stories of diverse and powerful people from around the world, I found similar struggles and triumphs that I wanted to know more about. As I analyzed the stories of my own life and the recurring themes within them, I realized that I earnestly desired to embody the power, love, and sound mind that my mom had instilled in me. Externally, I was striving to make this a reality, but something was still missing. I aimed to expand my capacity to navigate fear, shame, and the other human emotions because I desperately needed to manifest the life I dreamed of, which included coming to America, getting my degrees, and owning my own home. I thought all of these achievements would give me some degree of control and make me feel connected, but I still felt disconnected. Something was still missing after attaining the goals.

After much soul-searching, I realized that my achievements were not just for myself but were to serve as a platform for me to serve others in a leadership capacity. The missing connection was that, for me to unreservedly love, lead, and serve others, I first had to choose to embrace vulnerability and own my story. If I couldn't own my story, then I couldn't share myself authentically and serve others. Embracing vulnerability became a choice and practice for me. Additionally, the tough lesson I continue to learn every day in my pursuit of expressing power, love, and a sound mind is that no matter how much I understand myself as an evolving being, loving all of me is crucial for my authentic expression in the world. My life had been akin to the many graduation gowns collected in the closet, the albums filled with curated memories, and the polished, perfected projection of my life onto the world and those around me. The more I leaned into the emotional pain of my experiences, granting myself grace while integrating the parts of me I didn't like, the lighter, more connected, and empowered I began to emerge. Cultivating spiritual practices that resonated with my soul also became essential to my journey.

Tips for Your Own Vulnerability Journey, Part One:

A. Embark on the asking journey method.

B. Accept embracing vulnerability as a choice and practice.

C. Adapt spiritual practices that resonate with your soul. This could be silence, meditation, journaling, or study.

*"When we have the courage to walk into our story and own it.
We get to write the ending. And when we don't own our stories
of failure, setback, and hurt—they own us."*

~Brene Brown

My back story

During The Shadow Process hosted by The Ford Institute (Debbie Ford), which my then boyfriend, now husband, attended in 2011, I underwent a painful yet profoundly liberating moment of awakening. In one of our guided visualization meditations, we were instructed to recall a defining childhood moment. While in meditation, my 11-year-old self-emerged, consumed by the shame after not seeing my name listed in the national common entrance exam results.

Children growing up on the island of Jamaica are required to take an exam that determines their placement in high school. This exam, mandated for all fifth and sixth graders, allows each student to select their top two school choices. Today, things have changed somewhat in Jamaica. It is the dream of every child on the island to attend their preferred school, and we all anxiously await the summer months for the results to be published in the national newspaper. Typically, the Ministry of Education announces the date for publishing results, prompting parents to rise before dawn to purchase a copy of the newspaper.

I had not passed the exam. In my mind's eye, little Shakira scanned every name on the list of thousands of children, under every school, searching for her own name. There was no one around to offer comfort or encouragement.

That day, I interpreted my absence from the list as a sign that I didn't belong, I wasn't connected, and I wasn't worthy or smart enough. Little Shakira got up from the floor and walked out into the world trying to look perfect. If things at least looked perfect, there would be no questions asked, and she would not have to relive this sad and painful day.

At 11 years old, I understood that if I let anyone into my world, they would discover the truth. The shame of not passing that exam thrived in the secret, guarded cage of my heart. By staying in the background or remaining silent when given the chance to speak up, I ensured no one would discover that my name was missing—"I wasn't smart or good enough."

Here's the lie she told herself: She believed that by excelling at everything she pursued, accomplishing the dreams of her life, and hiding the shame from everyone, she would be safe. For 25 years, I never felt safe, worthy, accomplished, or connected.

The guided meditation gifted me with the insight to identify this defining moment from my 11-year-old self when hiding parts of myself or my story became necessary. Revisiting this memory marked a turning point in my journey on what it means to experience the vulnerability of presenting my authentic, imperfect self to the world.

The person I thought I should be was driven by the experiences of my 11-year-old self. To stand in power, love, lead, and serve, my 11-year-old self needed to grow up and be nurtured with tender care and self-acceptance.

Tips for Your Own Vulnerability Journey, Part Two:

Some of the tools I use to nurture and accept myself to this day are:

1. Engage in shadow work to get clear on your story. What parts of yourself do you like and dislike? Shadow work will support you in graciously owning all of you—your humanity and your divinity.

2. Practice positive self-talk, acts of self-love, self-compassion, and self-forgiveness as you move through owning your story.

3. Joining a community that supports your personal and professional development. For me, this is Toastmasters International and my spiritual community.

If you follow these tips, or begin to create your own, you will start to elevate and empower yourself beyond your current circumstances through the power of vulnerability. There are a variety of ways to nurture and accept yourself; there is no one-size-fits-all method. The key is to remember that the answers are within you, and finding these answers will give you access to creating a better life.

Vulnerability

noun - the quality or state of being exposed to the possibility of being attacked or harmed, either physically or emotionally.

"Vulnerability is not weakness; it's our greatest measure of courage."

~Brene Brown

The myth of vulnerability that leaves us disconnected from each other is that it is a sign of weakness. I have discovered that embracing vulnerability is about being connected to myself and, therefore, being able to connect to others. Yes, vulnerability is uncomfortable, but it is necessary for the journey of living authentically. It can leave you feeling naked, but you are not going to die. At 11 years old, I decided to shut down being exposed (vulnerable) to protect myself from shame. However, shame and disconnection were the results of my experience. The thoughts that dominated my mind—"I don't belong," "I am not worthy," and "I'm not smart or good enough"—simply grew in all areas of my life.

Without uprooting the negative beliefs from your consciousness by shining light on them, you end up never feeling good enough, even when you are standing in magnificent, life-changing opportunities.

The only way to heal yourself and share your gifts and talents with the world is to embrace vulnerability, open your heart, and expose your shame (of imperfections). The choice is either to take back your power and live fulfilled or be closed off and controlled by shame. Allow light to shine on the human experiences that make you unique, brilliant, different, flawed, and beautiful. From this space, you will find that you have more in common with others than you are different from them. The way to feel whole and fulfilled (an internal state) in your life is to take the most courageous step you will ever take: owning your story, sharing your story, and choosing to live authentically.

Courage

Noun – the ability to do something that frightens one.

Another way of defining courage is deciding to take a risk without knowing the outcome. The courageous acts we take each day to let ourselves be seen and heard and connect with each other build our muscle of courage.

Let's go back to The Shadow Process in 2011. Our Guide continued to create a safe space for us to delve deeper into meditation. She wanted us to reconnect with ourselves as children under the age of 10. As I relaxed and allowed the experience to unfold, I felt my eyes pop open from sleep. I had awakened in meditation as myself under the age of one. I knew I was this age because my body was that of a baby, and I was wearing a nappy (cloth diaper). I looked to the side and saw everyone running from the room. I couldn't follow them. I looked up and saw a thief coming through the window right above me. In absolute terror, I closed my eyes tightly and felt what I would describe as, "Do not move; it's not safe here, and people are not to be trusted."

This experience rocked me to the core. The unknown fear I felt living my life was confirmed. The disconnection and sense of not belonging were also confirmed. Feeling the immense emotions of betrayal and anguish within myself under the age of one was very profound. An overflowing love of finding her was also present. There was a sense of calm that was reassuring—it gently said, "It is okay to open your eyes and come out from the corner now." There was a sigh of relief that felt like I could finally breathe. Let me be very clear that it took months of journaling and talking through the memory of this experience with my mother to unpack and find the language to best describe the emotions. In unlocking the emotions accurately, I gained understanding and context, which ultimately led to me owning another piece of my story.

I left San Diego in 2011, never to be the same again. When I met my 11-year-old self, it was as though I was looking at her, but when I met myself under the age of one, I was looking through her eyes. Both stories shared with you represent an intimate part of my journey in embracing vulnerability and courageously pursuing my purpose in the world. My purpose is to encourage transformation and inspire divine connection within myself and others.

When you embrace authenticity, you feel shame and fear, yet you move forward anyway. How do you live healthily with shame?

1. Choose connection over isolation. Share your story and give others permission to lovingly do the same in your presence. Share your story with people who will honor and not judge you.

2. Recognize your triggers of shame. If your trigger is activated, breathe and drop from your head space to your heart. Create a sense of safety within yourself.

3. Practice gratitude for your imperfections. Live from the space of becoming, rather than reaching a destination. When you allow yourself to always be in the process of becoming, you lighten the weight of the need to be perfect. You release unnecessary expectations and instead focus on continual growth.

In authenticity, life becomes more fulfilling in collaboration rather than isolation. The measure of success due to interconnectedness is much grander than what you could ever create alone. If connecting, collaboration, or cooperation are experiences you want to enjoy, then take to heart the famous African proverb that says, "If you want to go fast, go alone. If you want to go far, go together," and practice it.

People frequently ask, "How do you know when you are being transformed?" The answer is when your perception of who you are begins to shift. Through the lens of this new perception, your life starts showing up differently. Keep in mind that transformation is ongoing and not a destination. You will know you are being transformed when your future is filled with possibilities and not tied to the past and when you take on the mantle of 100% responsibility for your life.

Embracing vulnerability and owning and sharing my story allowed me to tap into my own resilience and opened doors of impactful leadership positions where I can hold a mirror for others to see and own their greatness. I want you to know this is possible for you too.

If you desire to remove whatever is standing in the way of you living the life you desire, I encourage you to courageously take the steps to find the answers within yourself. Know that the right coach or mentor for you is someone who guides you back to your own answers, not someone who simply tells you what to do. Often, people shy away from introspection, but I implore you that wholeness and thriving lie within you. Embracing vulnerability makes it possible to love, lead, and serve authentically.

During the COVID-19 pandemic, I had the esteemed honor of leading a district within Toastmasters. At a time of great despair, personal and professional heartbreaks, sickness, and tremendous loss for everyone, I was elected to hold the number two position at the height of the pandemic and the number one position in 2021-2022. Out of a district of over 3,500 members, I was charged with overseeing and managing the district's day-to-day operations, finances, and human resources. Life offered me the opportunity to support and create a safe space for hundreds of people to be okay with not being okay. Our voices were heard, people felt seen, tears were shed, support was provided, and breakthroughs were celebrated weekly. With a team of 55 Toastmasters leaders, the vision was to reimagine leadership, recognize and honor each other, and rediscover our purpose in supporting each other in achieving our goals. The team of 55 went above and beyond expectations in serving the members of the district.

I am eternally grateful to my 11-year-old and under-1-year-old selves for the journey, courage, and capacity to serve in leadership during the pandemic. I believe that doing the self-work of owning and sharing these parts of my story prepared me to lead and serve during such a vulnerable and historic period and to become the leader I am today. Not all the leaders were comfortable with my style of heart-centered leadership, which requires a culture of embracing vulnerability, when we started the journey, but they leaned in nevertheless. Having walked the path of shared stories and embraced vulnerability together, not a month goes by today without some form of contact from a former team member who is reaping the rewards of embracing vulnerability in their lives.

In closing, a fulfilled life awaits the person who is brave enough to take a stand for authentic expression. If you desire to step into the possibility of living a different life—one that embraces who you are rather than who you think you should be—I challenge you to find the courage to own and share your story powerfully. It may not be comfortable or easy, but it will surely be worth your time and attention to obtain the wisdom and gifts from your story. Those who elevate themselves by embracing vulnerability will find that they ultimately empower themselves and others to engage with the world from a place of authenticity. The world needs the authentic you, so start the journey now.

Call to Action:

Go back through the chapter and capture the tips I shared with you. Below are three additional steps you can take to start or deepen your journey of living authentically:

1. Share something that demonstrates vulnerability. This could be a struggle, fear, or frustration.

2. Order and read *The Great Imperfection* by Brene Brown.

3. Order, read, and implement the practices of Debbie Ford's book *The Right Questions*.

About the Author

Having overcome shame, loneliness, and low self-esteem to the light of worthiness, confidence and empowered leader, Shakira's story qualifies her to inspire others to self-love, healing, and peace. Shakira Taylor is a Licensed Minister serving at The Universal Truth Center for Better Living in Miami Gardens, Florida. Shakira believes our real work on earth is to discover and express our true selves so we can give others permission to do the same. She explains "I believe that within our habits, labels, and experiences, lay the gifts we must share with the world. When we heal and own our story, we gain access to an internal power and strength that supports us in living purposefully. My purpose is to encourage transformation and inspire divine connection within myself and others.

At the center Shakira also serves as the platform lead chair, mentoring youth, and adults in honing their public speaking skills. As a prayer chaplain for over 10 years, she listens and holds sacred space with up to forty members monthly. She also teaches the Sunday lesson when called upon.

In addition, Shakira is a Distinguished Toastmaster. During the pandemic, she served as District Director for District 47, a region spanning Southeast Florida and the Bahamas. An elected position that is responsible for directly overseeing and managing the District's day-day operations, finance, and human resources. She led a team of fifty-five volunteers, completing her tenure as an award- winning District Director.

She is a Certified Shadow Coach, sought after conference speaker and mentor. She has worked in various business roles throughout her career. A graduate of Florida International University with a bachelor's degree in international business and marketing. She earned a master's degree in business administration from Nova Southeastern University.

Shakira is married to DEEP Transformation Coach and Senior Minister of Universal Truth Center for Better Living The Reverend Charles M. Taylor. They are co-founders of Charles & Shakira Unlimited, the catalyst for what they call the Healthy, Inspiring, Purposeful movement.

Connect with Shakira

LinkedIn: www.LinkedIn.com/in/shakiractaylor/

Facebook: Facebook.com/shakiractaylor

Quest For Cookies

By Jeff Katz

"So, what's wrong with her?" During the past twenty-one years, I have heard that question hundreds, maybe even thousands of times. "Hmmm, well...what is wrong with her?" The her in this case is my daughter Julia. She's a beautiful young lady who is twenty-one years old chronologically but only about eighteen months old developmentally. She loves music and splashing in water and cookies. Oh man, does she love cookies. Any flavor, any style, frosted, no frosting, it does not matter; she just loves cookies. She enjoys getting hugs and cuddles and kisses too. But wait, those are the things that are right with her. So what is wrong with Miss Julia Katz? Well, I'd again have to point out her severe developmental disabilities for the top of that list. I'd better mention that she cannot read, write, count, walk steadily, easily navigate steps, or discern what is hot, sharp, or dangerous. Oh, there are a few more limitations, too. If you really care to know, she can't take care of any of her personal activities of daily living either. Nope, Julia does not have the ability to wash herself, brush her teeth, use the toilet, make a sandwich, or clean up after herself, but she's still the most inspirational person I know.

How so, Jeff? She seems cute enough, but how can a young woman who does not have the ability to blow her nose teach me anything at all? In the most basic (and tasty) of terms, it's all about finding your cookie!

My wife, Heidi, and I had read all of the books that you get when your friends and family find out that you're going to become parents. "What to Expect When You're Expecting" and every variation on that theme. The nursery was painted, we had a load of diapers, an extensive wardrobe for the little prince, and proper baby-proofing had been done throughout the house. We knew exactly what we were getting into. We were confident and laser-beam focused. Harry did not disappoint in any way at all. Nope, the little guy was hitting every single one of his developmental milestones like nobody's business. Turning over, responding to sounds, crawling, feeding himself, etc. You name it, and that kid was ahead of the curve. Doing everything ahead of schedule. Even as a little guy, we were just sure that he'd be headed to the Ivy League eventually.

About two years into our run as self-proclaimed "parents of the year" to the boy we were sure must have been the most amazing kid ever, Julia arrived. Of course, we were old pros now. Heidi and I had this entire childbirth thing down to a tee. We were ready to expand the team. All we were waiting for was Julia's arrival.

That March morning, I started the day by heading to QVC in West Chester, Pennsylvania. I, along with a thousand other folks, had an audition to try and become a new host for the twenty four hour shopping channel. It was a pretty cool process, actually. Each of us had to bring an item with us and then proceed to present it to the network's executives. My show and tell was a banana! While I was standing in line, waiting my turn, I got a call from Heidi. She told me that she was pretty sure that she was having some contractions. OK, no problem, I'll head home now I told her. Nope, no need to miss the audition, she said, they are not close enough that we need to get to the hospital now she said. She assured me that she'd call again when we needed to bug out. I'll never really know if my successful audition was because I felt the added pressure of another little Katz arriving or not, but I successfully passed round one of the QVC audition process. The second and third parts of the QVC story play major roles in one of the keynote speeches I deliver entitled "Lessons from the Worst Salesman Ever!" and it is truly one of my favorites. A special gift for you is the knowledge that I was, in fact, offered the job!

With the audition wrapped up, I headed home to Heidi. Hospital bag, a few phone calls, and we were ready to go. A longtime friend of Heidi was watching Harry and we announced that we'd soon be back home with our new baby girl.

I may be biased, but I thought that Julia was beautiful as a newborn, and I believe she's still gorgeous today. I sat and gazed at Julia, seemingly for hours. Harry was moving around the house, marking off milestone after milestone ahead of the books' schedules. It was clear that he was just off the proverbial charts, but Julia, well Julia, was not hitting any of the milestones she was supposed to according to the same books. Roll over? No she seemed perfectly content as she was, whether it was on her tummy or on her back. Reaching for things? No, not really. Trying to feed herself or attempting to hold on to a toy of any sort? Nope. She was beautiful, but it seemed that was it for now.

As Heidi and I began to sense that there was something not quite right, friends and family members, motivated by all of the right reasons assured us repeatedly that she was "just on her own schedule" and urged us not to worry. Each time we heard that, we wound up worrying more and more. With our many sleepless nights already taking a toll on each of us, Heidi discovered what looked like a small hole, a dimple really, just above Julia's tush. The internet was somewhat primitive at the time, but we began researching what it could be. Spina bifida occulta seemed to be the answer, and it was confirmed at our next visit with the pediatrician. At that appointment, the doctor told us that some tests needed to be done. Little did we know that's when Julia's adventure through the medical world would begin. That kid has now been poked and prodded more in her two-decades-long life than I've been in almost sixty years. She's actually been more examined than anyone that I know, come to think of it. "Oh, wait, hang on for a minute, Mr. and Mrs. Katz, let me take a look at Julia's hair," the doc said as we were beginning to leave.

Sure, I thought to myself, let's take a look at Julia's hair. It's blonde, it's soft and it is beautiful. The doctor was not interested in any of that. Instead, he provided a brief lesson on genetics and chromosomal abnormalities. "Do you see how it spirals out? It starts in the center of her scalp. That is not where most people's hair starts. Yours, mine, the nurse's hair all starts off center and spirals out from there," he said. All of a sudden, the doctor's tone seemed much more intense than before. We'll need to get her to a geneticist, a chromosomal expert, and a DNA expert. "You also see how her eyes are not focusing on the same thing, and her nose is kind of flattened? Yes, you've got to get her down to some experts at Children's Hospital of Philadelphia," were the words we heard from him as we left his office.

After rounds of tests and exams, here's what we learned. Julia has severe global developmental disabilities and delays. The experts could not tell us exactly what was at the root of all of this, but in rather hushed and clinical tones, they told us that we should expect Julia would never crawl, let alone walk. She'd always need care and might even need to be placed in a facility of some sort. And that was that. Oh, we continued to bring her to all sorts of specialists through the years, but we were determined that she would live the best life she possibly could. Soon, she had a younger brother in addition to her older brother.

With Joe's arrival, we now had two typically developing boys and one severely disabled girl. Joe may be younger than Julia, but she'll always be the baby. It was, at times, crushing to see Joe hitting his developmental mileposts while Julia stayed at exactly the same level. I must confess that I've always told the boys that I love each of my children the same, but I do love Julia the most! Harry and Joe have rolled their eyes and grimaced at that for years, but it is kind of true.

Julia would never turn over we were told, but she did. She would never crawl, they said, but she did. In fact, the very first time that she did some exploring on her palms and knees, pulling herself in the most primitive of crawls, her brothers started clapping and cheering. Eventually, with the help of some leg braces, dedicated therapists, and thousands of hours of practice, she started to walk. "Frankensteiny" is how I would describe her gait, but she was still walking.

You're a good person and a kind one at that, right? You've read Julia's story up to this point. You may find it sad or joyful, but inspiring is what I pray that you take from all of this. There are certainly plenty of things that Julia will never do, that is true. She's never going to attend college, vote, or get her driver's license. Heidi will never enjoy a spa adventure with her. I will never get the opportunity to embarrass her by dancing with her at her wedding. So, you rightly ask, where's that inspiration you promised?

Earlier, I mentioned Julia's love of cookies. Does she have a favorite? Yes, whatever one she is busy eating. Chocolate, vanilla, peanut butter, oatmeal with raisins, oatmeal without raisins, iced, non-iced, round, square...it does not matter. If it is a cookie, she can identify it and she wants to eat it. She only understands a few words, and it will surely come as no surprise that one of the words she does know is cookie!

On a regular day, after Julia had returned home from school, her quest for cookies was presented in a way never before seen by us. She had always swiped at cookies that we were holding near her, but that was the limit. So, on this regular day, after Julia had enjoyed a snack and a cup of juice, been changed, and walked back to her safe and secure space, Heidi started to get dinner ready while I was working in my home office.

Heidi had set up our Ron Popeil rotisserie on the deck outside of the kitchen and she was ready to set it and forget it. Now you understand why I was so anxious to audition for that QVC job! A few minutes later, I heard a scream from Heidi. "Jeff, now, come here now! Right now!" she shouted. I got there as quickly as I could and saw an amazing sight.

Seated in the middle of the kitchen floor was Julia. Surrounding her on all sides, in every direction, was a sea of partially eaten cookies! It took me a moment to really process what was going on, and even as I was attempting to figure it all out, Julia was still at it. She would reach out to the cookies on the floor, pick one out, bring it to her mouth, take a single bite, and then toss it in the air. She did that over and over before I could get to her.

We've always used a secure baby gate to keep Julia safely in her space. Locked and secured with extra parts. It's often been confusing for us to get it open. Somehow this girl, with a baby's intellect, a toddler's cognitive ability, figured out exactly how to unlock that gate and open it in the right direction. Then, unaided and not wearing the AFO braces on her legs, she navigated through a bedroom, hallway, living room with steps, and a dining area before entering the kitchen.

Julia does not understand steep, uneven, hot, or sharp. She made her way around obstacles and avoided the knife drawer, stovetop, and oven. She knew that what she wanted was contained in our pantry... the cookies.

She opened the pantry doors and did not take anything else out. All the soups, spices, breads, bags of flour, and boxes of raisins were left untouched. Our very own version of The Cookie Monster was on a mission, it was to be the culmination of her quest for cookies. We learned that we had a lot of cookies in that pantry. Oatmeal, chocolate chip, sugar, lemon, Oreos, vanilla Oreos, double-stuffed Oreos, and Julia's absolute favorite, rainbow cookies from the Ukrop's bakery. I also spotted some crumbs that I did not recognize in the collection of cookie dust on the floor, so I've missed some of the flavors, I guess. It was an absolute mess, but man, what a totally glorious mess!

If this girl can assemble a priority list, designate an ultimate goal, and figure out how to navigate what is in her way, then there is no reason at all that you cannot do the same! If your cognitive state is greater than a toddler's, then you can do it...whatever that it is. Increased sales? Successful job search? Losing weight? Enhancing your personal relationships? These sound like delicious goals. Not crunchy or iced, but delicious nonetheless.

When you take some inspiration from Julia's quest for cookies, you will find that there is nothing out of your reach. Julia can't speak or write, but I believe that her quest for cookies was SMART...specific, measurable, attainable, relevant, and timely! Figure out what your cookie is, get it and start munching.

About the Author

Jeff Katz is known to many people for many reasons. Some know the Philadelphia native as a former police officer, some remember him from the world of professional wrestling, others have read his work as a columnist for The Boston Herald while plenty of folks enjoy his award winning shows on radio and television. But Jeff's greatest pride comes from being a father to three children.

The journey for both of his sons has been rather typical but his daughter's has been filled with special challenges. Julia recently turned 21 but she'll always be a toddler in many ways because of her global disabilities and special needs. Jeff is a well respected public speaker and coach who is in high demand around the country for his keynote speeches including his favorite entitled "Julia's Quest for Cookies" that details how Julia with the developmental age of 18 months successfully makes her way from the safety of her room to the kitchen pantry where she samples every single cookie!

Connect with Jeff

LinkedIn: LinkedIn.com/in/jeffreyakatz

Facebook: Facebook.com/coachjeffkatz

Website: www.JeffKatz.us

Conclusion

As we reach the end of this inspiring journey through *Elevate and Empower*, we hope you've found wisdom, strength, and practical strategies to navigate your own path of growth and resilience. The stories and insights shared by our contributors demonstrate that while life's challenges are universal, so too is our capacity to overcome them.

Each chapter in this anthology offers a unique perspective on personal transformation, but collectively they underscore a powerful truth: within each of us lies the potential to rise above adversity, to learn, to grow, and to inspire others along the way.

As you close this book, we encourage you to reflect on the lessons that resonated most deeply with you. Consider how you might apply these insights to your own life, career, or relationships. Remember, the journey of personal growth is ongoing, and each step forward, no matter how small, is a victory worth celebrating.

Perhaps reading these stories has ignited a spark within you – a desire to share your own experiences and wisdom with the world. If you've ever dreamed of writing a book or contributing to an anthology like this one, we'd love to hear from you. At Prominence Publishing, we're passionate about helping aspiring authors bring their visions to life and make a positive impact through the written word.

To learn more about how we create best-selling authors and to schedule a call with our team, visit:

Prominencepublishing.com/how-we-create-best-selling-authors.

Whether you're inspired to write, to lead, or simply to live with greater purpose and resilience, we hope this anthology has provided you with the tools and motivation to take that next step. Remember, your story matters, and your journey of growth and empowerment has the power to elevate not only your own life but the lives of those around you.

Thank you for joining us on this transformative journey. Now, go forth and elevate your world!